THE SAGA OF
DARREN SHAN
HUNTERS OF THE DUSK

VOLUME
7

Story: Darren Shan
Manga: Takahiro Arai

A SUMMARY OF THE VAMPIRE PRINCE:

DARREN EXPOSED KURDA'S TREACHERY AND BRILLIANTLY FOUGHT OFF AN IMPENDING VAMPANEZE ATTACK. BEFORE HIS EXECUTION, HOWEVER, KURDA ANNOUNCED THE ARRIVAL OF THE DREAD VAMPANEZE LORD, PROPHESIED TO DESTROY THE VAMPIRE RACE. WITH KURDA'S EXECUTION, A TERRIBLE WAR OVER THE FATE OF VAMPIRES AND VAMPANEZE HAD BEGUN. DUE TO HIS BRAVERY AND CUNNING, DARREN WAS AWARDED THE RANK OF VAMPIRE PRINCE. SIX YEARS LATER...

HUNTERS OF THE DUSK
CONTENTS

IT WAS AN AGE OF TRAGIC MISTAKES.

WHEN THE SPIDER BIT MY BEST FRIEND STEVE...

...I WAS FORCED TO ABANDON MY HUMANITY IN ORDER TO SAVE HIS LIFE.

FOR ME, THE TRAGEDY BEGAN FOURTEEN YEARS EARLIER...

...WHEN I STOLE THE AMAZING PERFORMING TARANTULA, MADAM OCTA, FROM HER VAMPIRE OWNER.

...BY TRAVELLING THE WORLD AS AN ASSISTANT TO MR. CREPSLEY, A BLOOD-DRINKING CREATURE OF THE NIGHT.

I PAID FOR MY CRIME...

MY NAME IS DARREN SHAN...

...AND I'M HALF-HUMAN, HALF-VAMPIRE.

CHAPTER 55:
WAR COUNCIL

THIS
IS MY
STORY.

THERE, I UNDERTOOK THE TRIALS OF INITIATION IN ORDER TO PROVE THAT I WAS WORTHY OF BEING CONSIDERED A FULL-FLEDGED VAMPIRE...

ON OUR TRAVELS AROUND THE WORLD, MR. CREPSLEY AND I STOPPED BY VAMPIRE MOUNTAIN.

IN FACT, KURDA WAS IN LEAGUE WITH THEM.

BUT ALONG THE WAY, WE RAN INTO A GROUP OF VAMPANEZE!

MY FRIENDS KURDA AND GAVNER HAD TO HELP ME ESCAPE SO THAT I WOULDN'T BE PUT TO DEATH.

...BUT I FAILED!

THEY'RE BOTH DESCENDED FROM THE SAME RACE, BUT THERE IS ONE MAJOR DIFFERENCE WITH THE VAMPANEZE.

THE PURPLE-SKINNED VAMPANEZE ARE NATURAL ENEMIES OF THE VAMPIRES.

...THEY ALWAYS KILL THE VICTIM.

WHEN THEY DRINK THE BLOOD OF THEIR HUMAN PREY...

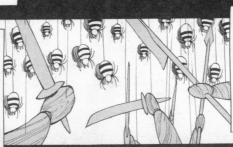

BUT WHEN I REVEALED THE TREACHERY THAT HAD TAKEN PLACE, THAT FRAGILE PEACE WAS SHATTERED.

WHILE THERE WAS NO LOVE LOST BETWEEN VAMPANEZE AND VAMPIRES, AN UNEASY TRUCE HAD KEPT THE TWO AT PEACE FOR HUNDREDS OF YEARS.

KATA

KATA

KATA

THAT THE VAMPANEZE LORD HAD FINALLY ARISEN!!

KATA (CLATTER)

KATA

...WE BECAME AWARE OF A TERRIBLE TRUTH.

IN THE END, WE DEFEATED THE BAND OF VAMPANEZE INSIDE THE MOUNTAIN, BUT DURING THE TRAITOR KURDA'S QUESTIONING...

SUCH WAS THE PROPHECY MADE BY MR. TINY SEVEN HUNDRED YEARS AGO.

"AND HE WILL LEAD THE VAMPANEZE AGAINST US, AND WIPE THE VAMPIRES FROM THE FACE OF THE EARTH."

THERE WOULD BE NO FUTURE FOR VAMPIRE-KIND UNLESS THEY COULD DESTROY THE LORD BEFORE HIS RISE TO POWER.

VAMPANEZE ACROSS THE WORLD WERE PREPARING FOR THE VIOLENT, BLOODY WAR THAT WOULD COME.

...WOULD FOREVER BE KNOWN AS THE "WAR OF THE SCARS."

A BATTLE THAT, DUE TO THE MARKS ON THE FINGERTIPS OF BOTH VAMPIRE AND VAMPANEZE...

THUS, AFTER THE PASSING OF KURDA, THE BATTLE FOR THE SURVIVAL OF OUR RACES BEGAN.

SIRE SHAN!

SPEAK!

SIX YEARS AFTER KURDA'S DEATH.

ALREADY IT HAS BEEN FOURTEEN YEARS SINCE MY BLOODING AS A HALF-VAMPIRE.

HEAR ME, SIRE SKYLE!

I BRING REPORTS OF BATTLE!

...WHILE KURDA WAS KILLED WHEN HE SHOULD HAVE BEEN A PRINCE IS AN IRONY THAT ISN'T LOST ON ME.

THE FACT THAT I HAVE BECOME A PRINCE WHEN I SHOULD HAVE BEEN KILLED...

...I WAS MADE ONE OF THE FIVE VAMPIRE PRINCES WHO RULE OVER THE VAMPIRE RACE.

IN RECOGNITION OF MY DEFEAT OF THE VAMPANEZE ...

TWO YEARS AGO, I EVEN ATTEMPTED THE TRIALS I HAD FAILED EARLIER AND PASSED THEM EASILY.

IN MY PAST SIX YEARS AS A PRINCE, I'VE STAYED ON VAMPIRE MOUNTAIN, CULTIVATING MY KNOWLEDGE AND STRENGTH.

LET US OBSERVE WITH THE STONE OF BLOOD.

I SEE.

...BASED ON SEVERAL EYEWITNESS ACCOUNTS OF VAMPANEZE IN THAT AREA!

I HAVE A GROUP OF FOUR GENERALS SCOUTING A STRATEGIC LOCATION...

IT DETERMINES THE FATE OF THE VAMPIRE RACE.

THE STONE OF BLOOD IS A MAGICAL ARTEFACT OF MANY SECRETS.

SFX: BA (WHOOSH)

THROUGH THE USE OF TELEPATHY, WARRIORS CAN BE ORDERED ABOUT AND STRATEGIES PUT INTO MOTION.

...THE LOCATIONS OF THE NEARLY THREE THOUSAND VAMPIRES SCATTERED ABOUT THE WORLD.

THE STONE OF BLOOD WILL TELL ITS USER...

DARREN.

...

I SEE...

SUU (SHH)

NAME OF THE CITY? WHAT ABOUT IT...?

BUT HAVE YOU SEEN THE NAME OF THE CITY?

YES. MY ORIGINAL HOME.

OH! WHERE WE FOUND MUR-LOUGH!!

HAVE YOU SEEN THIS, DARREN?

WELL, IT LOOKS LIKE WE'VE ENGAGED IN MANY SKIRMISHES WITH THE VAMPANEZE IN THIS AREA.

I CANNOT SEE WHY. IT IS NOT A LOCATION OF ANY IMPORTANCE.

WHAT COULD IT MEAN? HAVE THE VAMPANEZE MADE A BASE THERE?

HAVE YOU ANY WORD OF THE VAMPANEZE LORD'S WHERE-ABOUTS?

MOVING ON...

...

WE HAVEN'T EVEN THE SLIGHTEST CLUE YET...

STILL NONE, SIRE.

YOU MAY GO.

A SHAME... BUT YOUR WORK IS APPRECIATED.

FRESH NEWS!!

WE HAVE REPORTS, SIRE!

MMM...

ZAWA (MURMUR)

ZAWA

ARIS!

FURA (SLUMP)

BUT YOU ARE NOT, SIRE.

DON'T BE A FOOL. THE NIGHT IS STILL YOUNG.

PERHAPS YOU SHOULD CALL IT A NIGHT.

HERE

SFX: GOKU (GULP)

...YET AS MY GUARDIAN, HE UNOFFICIALLY HAS ALL THE POWERS OF A PRINCE.

HE IS AN ORDINARY VAMPIRE WITH NO RECOGNISABLE RANK...

MR. CREPSLEY IS IN A PECULIAR POSITION.

I AM ON MY LAST LEGS.

AN OLD OWL HATES TO BE TOLD HOW YOUNG AND VIRILE HE IS.

BUT...

NON-SENSE!

YOU SHOULD REST, PARIS.

I WISH TO MAKE MY MARK NOW, WHILE I STILL CAN.

YOU AN' DARREN ARE TH' FUTURE LARTEN

WILL DAR-REN BE ABLE TO MANAGE WITHOUT ME?

DARREN WILL MANAGE.

BUT THIS *HAS* BEEN A TAXING NIGHT.

...IS A FOOL, A LIAR, OR BOTH.

ANYONE WHO SAYS OTHERWISE...

I SHOULD HOPE NOT.

VERY WELL. I WILL NOT ARGUE WITH YOU.

MR. CREPSLEY AND I REMAINED BEHIND TO CONTINUE THE MEETING.

MANIPULA-TION OF THE STONE OF BLOOD HAD LEFT PARIS COMPLETELY EXHAUSTED.

THERE'S GOT TO BE SOME-THING THERE!

SURELY YOU ARE NOT SUGGESTING THAT WE VENTURE THERE NOW!

ABOUT YOUR HOME-TOWN... I THINK WE SHOULD CHECK IT OUT...

SAY, MR. CREPS-LEY...

A PRINCE DOES NOT RUN ABOUT ON HIS OWN WHIM.

DO NOT PLACE YOUR OWN CONCERNS AHEAD OF THE CLAN'S.

WE HAVEN'T TAKEN A SINGLE STEP OUT OF THIS MOUNTAIN IN SIX YEARS.

WELL, IF I HAD A GOOD TEACH-ER...

HMPH!

WHEN WILL YOU FINALLY REACH THE AGE WHERE I NO LONGER NEED WATCH OVER YOUR EVERY MOVE?

YOU ARE SUCH A MEDDLESOME LITTLE BRAT, EVEN AFTER ALL THESE YEARS.

HA HA...

HA HA HA...

...THERE WAS NOTHING ABOUT THE VAMPANEZE LORD.

DESPITE THE MANY REPORTS I HAD TO WADE THROUGH THAT EVENING...

AH...

AHH ...

YOU'RE ALL RIGHT, YOU'RE SAFE! GET A GRIP, HARKAT!

DRAGONS!!!

BATA

BATA (THUMP)

SORRY, DARREN...

YOU'VE JUST BEEN DREAMING.

THERE ARE NO DRAGONS HERE.

...AND THEN THE DRAGONS ATTACKED...

YES. I WAS WANDERING IN A VAST WASTELAND...

WAS IT THE SAME NIGHTMARE AGAIN?

...THOUGH I THINK THEY'D HAVE APPEARED IF YOU...HADN'T WOKEN ME UP.

NOT THIS TIME...

BASA (FLAP)

WERE THE SHADOWY MEN THERE?

GUI (TUG)

AND WITH MIKA AND ARROW OUT DOING BATTLE...

BUT I CAN'T LEAVE PARIS TO DEAL WITH IT ALONE.

I KNOW. THIS WAR BUSINESS IS KILLING ME.

IT'S BEEN AGES SINCE... WE GOT TOGETHER.

IT'S GOOD TO SEE YOU, DARREN.

GU (SQUEEZE)

HOW IS SIRE SKYLE?

...I NEED TO MAKE MYSELF AS USEFUL AS I CAN.

THERE ARE A MILLION THINGS THAT MUST BE DONE.

SO MANY VAMPIRES TO SEND TO THEIR DEATHS.

SO MANY DECISIONS TO MAKE AND TROOPS TO ORGANISE...

HE'S BEARING UP. BUT IT'S HARD.

EVERYONE SAYS YOU'RE FIT TO BE THE NEXT QUARTERMASTER OF THE MOUNTAIN, HARKAT.

PETA (PAT)

MANAGING FOOD, CLOTHES, WEAPONS, AND SO ON.

BUSY. SEBA'S BEEN WORKING ME HARDER ALL THE TIME.

HOW'VE YOU BEEN, HARKAT?

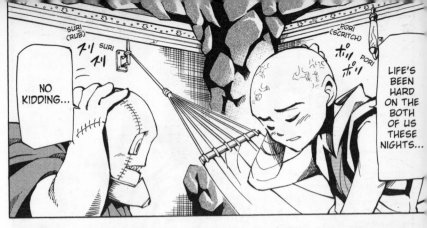

DARREN!

ZA (STOMP)

DO. SEBA WOULD BE DELIGHTED.

BUT I'LL TRY TO DROP BY SOON.

HURRY TO THE HALL OF PRINCES!

PRINCE MIKA VER LETH HAS RETURNED FROM BATTLE AFTER FIVE LONG YEARS!!

MIKA'S BACK!?

EVERYONE TO THE HALL OF PRINCES!!

I BRING NEWS OF THE VAMPANEZE LORD!!!

FIRST, LET'S MAKE IT CLEAR...

BUT WHAT'S THIS I HEAR ABOUT THE VAMPANEZE LORD?

I'M GETTING PLENTY OF HELP.

NOT BAD.

...I DON'T KNOW WHERE HE IS.

BUT I'VE HAD WORD OF HIM.

DOYO
(MURMUR)

ド゛ョ...

OH... THAT'S TOO BAD.

RE-CRUITS...

...YOU SAY?

BEFORE I BEGIN, DO YOU KNOW ABOUT THE LATEST VAMPANEZE RECRUITS?

IT IS NOTHING TO WORRY ABOUT. WE STILL OUT-NUMBER THEM GREATLY.

INCREAS-ING THEIR NUMBERS WAS ALWAYS A PART OF THEIR STRATEGY.

THIS IS OLD NEWS. WE EXPECTED THEM TO BLOOD RECKLESSLY.

SO YOU MIGHT THINK...

VAM-PETS, MIKA?

...BUT THESE NEW RECRUITS ARE CALLED "VAMPETS."

THEIR LORD PLANS TO BUILD AN ARMY OF HUMAN HELPERS.

THEY ARE UNBLOODED HUMANS WHO LEARN THE RULES OF VAMPANEZE LIFE AND WARFARE.

...WHAT DO YOU THINK OF THEM NOW?

HAH! I BELIEVE WE ARE CAPABLE OF DEALING WITH MERE HUMANS, SIRE!

NOR-MALLY, I WOULD QUITE AGREE.

BUT...

ZAWA (MURMUR)...

THE VAMPETS USE GUNS!!

ARE THOSE... BULLET WOUNDS, SIRE?

THEY ARE INDEED.

YES, AND THEY'RE EVEN STRICTER THAN US WHEN IT COMES TO USING WEAPONS AT ALL!

BUT THE VAMPANEZE ARE LIKE US—THEY HAVE IRONCLAD RULES AGAINST THE USE OF RANGED WEAPONS!

OOH!

...AND SQUEEZED SOME INTERESTING DETAILS OUT OF HIM.

I CAUGHT ONE OF THESE VAMPETS A FEW MONTHS AGO...

ON THE OTHER HAND, THEY ARE NOT AS HARDENED AS THE VAMPANEZE.

THEY ARE NOT BOUND BY THE HARSH LAWS OF OUR COUSINS.

BUT THE VAMPETS AREN'T VAMPANEZE.

...MOVING AMONG THE VARIOUS FIGHTING UNITS, KEEPING UP MORALE.

HE'S TRAVELLING THE WORLD WITH A SMALL BAND OF GUARDS...

FIRST, THE VAMPANEZE LORD DOESN'T HAVE A "BASE."

...AND DESPITE HIS EFFORTS, MORALE IS LOW.

I ALSO LEARNED THAT THE VAMPANEZE LORD STILL HASN'T BEEN BLOODED...

...HIS GUARD WILL BE THIN!

ZAWA

WE'LL HAVE ANY NUMBER OF WAYS TO BEAT HIM!

WELL, AS LONG AS WE CAN FIND OUT WHERE HE IS...

OOOOH!

...EVEN OUTRIGHT SURRENDER!

THERE HAS BEEN TALK OF A PEACE TREATY...

MANY DON'T BELIEVE THEY CAN WIN THE WAR.

WE MUST CELEBRATE!

OUR VICTORY IS AT HAND!

LONG LIVE SIRE MIKA!

IF THE VAM-PANEZE ARE CONSIDERING SURRENDER, WE SHOULD PUSH HARD AFTER THEM.

THIS IS FOOL-ISH.

WAAAH (RAHHH)

A TOAST!

WE DRINK!

SIRE!

GO WITH THEM, LARTEN.

GET YOURSELF GOOD AND STEAMING DRUNK.

I CAN AND DO, LARTEN. BESIDES, IT WOULD BE IMPOLITE TO LET MIKA AND HIS OVEREAGER COMPANIONS DRINK ALONE.

B-BUT YOU CANNOT SUGGEST—

THAT IS AN ORDER, LARTEN.

GO AND UNWIND, AND DO NOT RETURN WITHOUT A HANGOVER.

KA (TOK)

KA

AS YOU SAY, SIRE.

MMM?

IF I HAD TO DESCRIBE IT...

WHAT'S MR. CREPSLEY LIKE WITH A HANG-OVER?

...

TWO
MOONS
...

MOON
...

UHH
...

GREEN
?

HAVE
FUN LAST
NIGHT,
DARREN?

AAAH!
HARKAT!?

THAT'S
FUNNY.
YOU WERE
SINGING
ABOUT HOW
MUCH YOU...
LOVED IT
EARLIER.

AAGH!
IT'S
MORE
ALE!

OEEE
CURRGH!

MY
HEAD IS
KILLING
ME...

I FEEL
LIKE I'VE
BEEN
POISONED.

THANK
YOU...

HERE,
DRINK
THIS.

WHAT'S THE MATTER, HARKAT?

NOTHING... NOTHING'S WRONG. JUST FELT LIKE...

SOWA (FIDGET)

SOWA

I'D RATHER NOT PUKE, THANKS.

URP

JUST HAVING A BIT OF FUN... WITH YOU.

WANT ANYTHING TO EAT?

HA HA...

LUCKY YOU.

ALCOHOL HAS NO EFFECT ON ME. I DON'T KNOW... HOW IT IS.

WHAT? NO!

NOT THE SHOWERS! HAVE MERCY!

BASA (FLAP)

...THAT TAKING A SHOWER IN THE HALL OF PERTA VIN-GRAHL IS THE BEST WAY... TO CURE HANGOVERS!

NEVER MIND ANY OF THAT! SEBA TOLD ME...

YOU'LL FEEL BETTER!

DON'T SPLASH MORE ON ME, HARKAT!

ZAZAA (F.SHHH)

AAAAGH!!!

 THEY MUST HAVE DRAINED HALF THE... MOUNTAIN'S SUPPLY OF ALE LAST NIGHT.

 NOW THIS IS A DREAD-FUL SIGHT.

I... TOLD YOU.

 WHEW! I FEEL ABOUT A HUNDRED TIMES BETTER NOW!

 EVERYONE'S BEEN SO PENSIVE LATELY. THIS WAS PROBABLY A GOOD BREATHER FOR THEM.

THEY MUST HAVE BEEN HAPPY ABOUT THE NEWS MIKA BROUGHT.

 THERE HE IS! MR. CREPSLEY!

HE MUST HAVE HAD THREE TIMES THE ALE I DID...

 I WONDER WHERE MR. CREPSLEY WOUND UP?

 NNGH!

NO! YOU *DID!?*

I HEARD YOU SINGING LAST NIGHT.

HARKAT, DARREN!

SORRY TO INTERRUPT. AT EASE, MEN.

SIRE SHAN!

BISHI (HUP)

...TO HAVE ALE BANNED.

HA... I SHOULD USE MY AUTHORITY...

"I AM THE PRINCE, THE PRINCE OF ALE!" RIGHT?

HEH HEH!

"ALE, ALE, I DRINK LIKE A WHALE!" ♪

NO TIME. WE'RE PERPETUALLY SHORT ON GOOD FIGHTERS IN THIS WAR.

HAVE TO KEEP TRAINING REPLACEMENTS FOR THOSE WHO FALL.

WHY DIDN'T YOU JOIN US, VANEZ?

IT'S THE ONLY WAY TO HELP THEM SURVIVE...

I ONLY WISH I COULD TEACH THEM EVERYTHING I HAVE TO SHOW.

BUT WE ARE AT WAR.

THERE'S NOWHERE NEAR ENOUGH TIME TO TRAIN THEM.

JUST BETWEEN US, THEY'RE AS POOR A TRIO OF GENERALS AS I'VE EVER PASSED.

I WISH I COULD DO MORE TO HELP IN THE EFFORT.

SOUNDS LIKE EVERYONE ELSE IS RISKING THEIR LIVES OVER THIS FIGHT.

... THEN AGAIN ...

I'VE GOT WORK TO DO, BUT...

ARE YOU OKAY, HARKAT?

GUGU (STRETCH)

WELL, I GUESS IT'S TIME TO START PREPARING FOR THE NEXT MEETING!

YOU'LL COME!?

OUTSIDE SOUNDS NICE! LET'S GO!

I WANT TO GET OUT AND... MOVE MY BODY.

WHY DON'T WE GO OUTSIDE, DARREN?

SOWA (FIDGET)

SOWA

ARE YOU LISTEN-ING?

HEY, HAR-KAT?

KA'! GASHA (CLANK)

GARA (CCLUNK)

KA'!

I WAS JUST THINKING ABOUT HOW MUCH I'D ENJOY SOME FRESH AIR.

AAAH!

THIS FEELS GREAT!!

SFX: KYORO (SPIN) KYORO

WONDER IF STREAK OR RUDI ARE OUT THERE SOMEWHERE ...

MUST BE LATE AUTUMN OR EARLY WINTER.

IT'S COLD...

!!!!

YOU COULD HAVE TRIPPED AND CRACKED YOUR—

WHAT'S GOTTEN INTO YOU, HARKAT!?

LOOK OUT!!!

HARKAT!!

ミシ!!
(STARED)

IS SOMETHING... OUT THERE?

ズザザ
(ZRRSHH)

I THINK ALL THOSE DREAMS ARE GETTING TO YOUR HEAD.

DRAG-ONS AGAIN?

THE DRAG-ON MAS-TER...

WHO?

HE'S COMING...

C'MON, HARKAT. LET'S GO BACK INSIDE AND GET YOU SOME—

HELLO BOYS! ARE YOU THE WELCOMING COMMITTEE?

PLEASE LET IT ALL BE A MISTAKE.

AND YOU...

YOU'VE GROWN, YOUNG SHAN.

THAT... VOICE...

JITO (DRIP)

YOU HAVE CHANGED TOO... HARKAT MULDS. AS I ALWAYS KNEW YOU WOULD.

...I KNEW THAT HIS REAPPEARANCE MEANT NOTHING BUT TROUBLE.

BUT THE MOMENT I RECOGNISED MR. TINY...

POU
(GLOW)

SUU
(SHHK)

CHAPTER·57: CHOSEN·ONES

...AND IT HASN'T CHANGED THE TINIEST BIT.

SEVEN HUNDRED YEARS...

KA
(TOKK)

THE MEETING STARTED SEVERAL—

YOU ARE TARDY, DARREN!

IT'S STOOD THE TEST OF TIME QUITE WELL, HASN'T IT?

CHAPTER 57: CHOSEN ONES

ZAWA

ZAWA (MUTTER)

I DON'T KNOW. THE ONLY THING I'M SURE OF...

ZAWA

ZAWA

WHAT IS THE MEANING OF THIS, DARREN?

...IS THAT IT CAN'T BE ANYTHING GOOD.

THEN I'LL COME STRAIGHT TO THE POINT.

ALL PRESENT AND CORRECT?

HE LOOKS TERRIFIED.

POOR HARKAT.

SU (SSK)

WHAT'S HIS PURPOSE IN DOING THIS?

MR. TINY HAS CALLED ALL THE VAMPIRES INTO THE HALL OF PRINCES.

THE LORD OF THE VAMPANEZE HAS BEEN BLOODED!

NIYA CLEER!

NIYA

THE FUTURE IS BOTH OPEN AND CLOSED.

BUT IT IS NOTHING MORE THAN THE MOST LIKELY TRUTH AHEAD OF YOU.

...THAT THE VAMPANEZE LORD WOULD WIPE YOU OUT.

SEVEN HUNDRED YEARS AGO, I TOLD YOUR FORE-BEARS...

IF YOU FIND AND KILL HIM BEFORE HE'S FULLY BLOODED...

THE VAM-PANEZE LORD IS ONLY A HALF-VAM-PANEZE AT THE MOMENT.

OUT OF THE HUNDREDS OF "CAN BE'S" IN YOUR FUTURE...

...THERE ARE SOME IN WHICH THE VAMPANEZE LORD AND HIS FOLLOW-ERS CAN BE DEFEATED.

WA (CRAHH)

...VICTORY WILL BE YOURS!

OOOOO

OOOOO

OOOOO (RAHHHH)

NIYA
NIYA
NIYA!

...THERE'S GOING TO BE SUFFERING AND MISERY.

HE ONLY GRINS LIKE THAT WHEN HE KNOWS ...

MR. TINY ISN'T THE TYPE TO SMILE BROADLY WHEN DELIVERING GOOD NEWS.

HE'S ENJOYING OUR REACTION.

SFX: JITO (HALT)

...WAS KURDA SMAHLT.

DOYO (MURMUR)

THAT CHANCE...

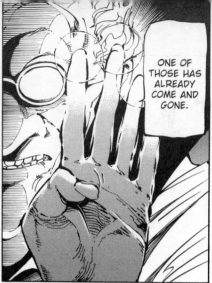

ONE OF THOSE HAS ALREADY COME AND GONE.

...AND THE WAR OF THE SCARS, AS YOU CALL IT, WOULD HAVE BEEN PREVENTED.

IF KURDA HAD SUCCEEDED, MOST VAMPIRES WOULD HAVE JOINED THE VAMPANEZE...

KURDA SMAHLT WAS A TRAITOR. I'D RATHER DIE HONOURABLY THAN OWE MY LIFE TO A TRAITOR.

BUT YOU KILLED HIM, DESTROYING WHAT WAS PROBABLY YOUR BEST HOPE OF SURVIVAL IN THE PROCESS. THAT WAS SILLY.

WHICH LEAVES...

...THREE FINGERS!

...SO WE SHALL IGNORE IT.

IT WILL NOT FALL FOR SOME TIME YET, IF AT ALL...

KOKI (CRIK)

MORE FOOL YOU.

THIS REPRESENTS YOUR LAST CHANCE, IF ALL OTHERS FAIL.

HIRA HIRA (SWISH)

HIRA

OH, DON'T MENTION IT.

YOU HAVE BEEN VERY GENEROUS WITH YOUR INFORMATION, DESMOND. I THANK YOU.

...POOF! IN THE NIGHT.

Bonk

...AND TELL US WHICH VAMPIRES ARE DESTINED TO ENCOUNTER THE VAMPANEZE LORD?

WILL YOU EXTEND YOUR GENEROSITY...

IF THE OTHERS HEAD FOR THE CAVE OF LADY EVANNA, THEY'LL PROBABLY RUN INTO HIM ALONG THE WAY.

DOKA (THUMP)

ONE OF THE HUNTERS IS ABSENT, SO I'LL NOT NAME HIM.

VERY WELL!

I THINK I KNOW WHAT'S COMING.

I'M GETTING THAT FEELING.

IN FACT, YOU MIGHT EVEN CALL THEM THE THREE LORD HUNTERS! RATHER CATCHY, DON'T YOU THINK?

THE HUNTERS MUST BE...

AND THE PAIR THAT IS PRESENT? THEY ARE...?

MM?

...AND HIS ASSISTANT, DARREN SHAN.

...LARTEN CREPSLEY...

I KNEW I WAS IN TROUBLE WHEN I SAW YOU SMILING.

OOH!

...HUNTERS!

MR. CREPSLEY AND I...

NOTHING ABOUT YOU SURPRISES ME...

YOU ARE NOT SURPRISED, MASTER SHAN?

FRIGHTENED, MASTER SHAN? WHAT IF YOU AREN'T ANY HELP?

WHAT COMES, WE TAKE.

WHAT IF YOU FAIL AND DAMN THE VAMPIRES TO EXTINCTION?

...WHEN YOU WERE *LESS* CLEVER.

I MUST SAY THAT I PRE-FERRED YOU...

WELL, YOU'VE LEARNED HOW TO SPEAK LIKE ONE.

THINK YOU MIGHT BREAK BENEATH IT?

I MIGHT.

YES.

SCARED BY THE WEIGHT OF YOUR RESPONSI-BILITIES?

WHAT ABOUT YOU, LARTEN?

AYE! ME TOO!

WHAT ABOUT THE REST OF US? I'VE SPENT FIVE YEARS HUNTING FOR THAT ACCURSED LORD!

YOU TWO ARE NO FUN. IT'S IMPOSSIBLE TO GET A RISE OUT OF YOU!

I WISH TO ACCOMPANY THEM!

AND ME!

...ABOUT THE MECH-ANISMS OF FATE?

...DARE TO TELL *ME*, WHO MEASURES TIME IN CONTINENTAL DRIFTS...

WOULD *YOU*, WHO HAS NOT SEEN *THREE* CENTURIES...

BIKI

PIKI (CRIK)

PACHIN

PACHIN

PITA (STOP)

I'M SORRY!!

BAGA (GRANK)

I DIDN'T MEAN TO OFFEND YOU!

NO! I APOLO-GIZE!

PARA

...AND ONLY THREE.

HAA

THERE ARE THREE HUNTERS...

HAA (CHUFF)

PARA (CRINKLE)

...BUT NO VAMPIRES SHOULD SEEK OUT THE HUNTERS. ALONE THEY MUST STAND TO SUCCEED OR FAIL.

NON-VAMPIRES MAY— INDEED, MUST— PLAY A PART IN THE HUNT...

...BUT WITH A SNAP OF HIS FINGERS —!

A THOUSAND VAMPIRES COULDN'T PUT A CRACK IN THESE WALLS...

GOOD! THEN WE'RE DECIDED!

KA-TOKKO

PARA

PARA

EVERYBODY WITHIN A TEN-MILE RADIUS WILL BE ROASTED ALIVE!

A VOLCANO'S DUE TO ERUPT ON A SMALL TROPICAL ISLAND TOMORROW.

BUT ENOUGH OF THE CHIT-CHAT, BOYS!

I WANT TO BE THERE— IT SOUNDS LIKE GREAT FUN.

GU (GRIT)

IF YOU COME WITH ME, I'LL REVEAL THE TRUTH OF YOUR FORMER IDENTITY. WILL YOU JOIN ME?

YOU HAVE DELIVERED MY MESSAGE AND SERVED YOUR PURPOSE ADMIRABLY.

YOU TOO, HARKAT!

...!!

...AND LARTEN.

I FEEL THAT I SHOULD GO WITH DARREN...

I HAVE A FEELING.

SOMETHING WHISPERS TO ME... HERE.

...I FEEL THAT MY PLACE IS WITH THE VAMPIRES. ALL ELSE CAN WAIT.

I'LL GO WITH THEM. RIGHT OR WRONG...

I THINK THAT IF I... LEAVE YOU TO LEARN THE TRUTH...

YOU'VE ALREADY SAVED MY LIFE TWICE.

HARKAT, YOU DON'T OWE US.

HARKAT...

...THE PERSON I WAS... WON'T LIKE WHAT I'VE DONE.

...AND LEARN THE TRUTH ABOUT YOURSELF.

GO WITH MR. TINY...

HOW-EVER, A WARN-ING.

IF YOU DO GO WITH THEM, YOUR PARTICIPATION COULD BE IMPORTANT IN DEFEATING THE VAMPANEZE LORD.

SO BE IT.

I DO SO HOPE TO SEE YOU AT THE FINAL CONFRON-TATION!

BEST OF LUCK TO YOU, DEAR VAMPIRES!

TRY NOT TO LET THE NIGHTMARES EAT YOU ALIVE.

HIRA

HIRA (SWISH)

WHAT IS IT?

I WANTED TO SHOW YOU SOMETHING BEFORE YOU LEFT ...

THIS.

...AND IT'S PATTERNED LIKE MADAM OCTA...

IT'S TOO LARGE TO BE A BA'HALEN'S SPIDER...

KASA (SCUTTLE)

I'VE NEVER SEEN THAT TYPE OF SPIDER BEFORE.

TWO DIFFERENT TYPES OF SPIDERS HAVE FOUND COMMON GROUND PEACEFULLY.

IT IS A WONDERFUL THING.

BA' SHAN'S SPIDERS ...?

PRECISELY!

YOU DON'T MEAN—!

AS COULD VAMPIRES AND VAMPANEZE ...

..IF THE GODS ARE ILLING.

I CALL THEM "BA'SHAN'S SPIDERS." I HOPE YOU DO NOT OBJECT.

MADAM OCTA MATED WITH BA'HALEN'S SPIDERS.

SEBA, THIS MAY NOT BE THE TIME OR PLACE...

BUT ONE THING IS CERTAIN: IF THE CHANCE TO KILL THE VAMPANEZE LORD FALLS TO ME, MY AIM WILL BE TRUE.

WHEN I LEAVE ON THIS JOURNEY...

...IT WILL BE TO DISCOVER WHAT IS RIGHT AND WHAT IS WRONG.

PERHAPS I HAVE GONE FEEBLE IN MY OLD AGE.

AH. FORGIVE THIS OLD VAMPIRE HIS MUTTERINGS.

...AND THE SAKE OF THE FUTURE.

FOR THE SAKE OF ALL VAMPIRES ...

AND INTO THE NIGHT WE WENT, LEAVING BEHIND THE SAFETY OF VAMPIRE MOUNTAIN.

OUR LONG, DARK HUNT FOR THE LORD OF THE VAMPANEZE HAD BEGUN.

CHAPTER 58:
CHANGES

FOLLOWING THE TRAIL MR. TINY HAD LEFT US, WE WERE ON OUR WAY TO LADY EVANNA'S CAVE...

IT HAD BEEN WEEKS SINCE WE LEFT VAMPIRE MOUNTAIN IN SEARCH OF THE VAMPANEZE LORD.

DELICIOUS! THIS IS THE LIFE, ISN'T IT?

MMM, I'M STARVING!

PACHI (SNAP)

PACHI

...AWAITING A POSSIBLE ENCOUNTER WITH THE THIRD HUNTER.

HAGU (CHOMP)

YOU ARE NOT IN A HURRY TO RETURN TO VAMPIRE MOUNTAIN?

HAFU (CHUFF)

HAFU

I WISH WE COULD GO ON LIKE THIS FOREVER.

YOU SPEAK OF THINGS YOU DO NOT UNDERSTAND.

BAH...

YOU CAN'T HIDE IT FROM ME.

COME ON, YOU KNOW YOU'RE HAPPY TO BE OUT ON THE ROAD AGAIN!

BEING A PRINCE IS A GREAT HONOUR, BUT IT'S NOT MUCH FUN.

YOUR TIMING WAS UNFORTU-NATE.

YOU HAVE HAD A ROUGH INITIATION, NOT TO MENTION THE MATTER OF THIS WAR.

PACHI

PACHI

I LOVED VAMPIRE MOUNTAIN... IT FELT LIKE HOME.

HARKAT'S BEEN IN A FUNK EVER SINCE WE LEFT.

TRY NOT TO LET THE NIGHTMARES EAT YOU ALIVE.

HE MUST BE WORRIED ABOUT WHAT MR. TINY SAID.

YOU COULD HAVE EVEN BEEN A PRINCE!

PERHAPS THERE IS VAMPIRE BLOOD IN YOU.

WHEN THIS IS OVER, IF I HAVE...THE CHOICE, I'LL RETURN.

I NEVER FELT SO AT EASE BEFORE EVEN WHEN I...WAS WITH THE CIRQUE DU FREAK.

...BUT ALSO A WITCH—

YES, AND NOT ONLY ARE THERE THE USUAL STAKES, DRAGONS, AND SHADOW MEN...

YOU HAVEN'T BEEN SLEEPING WELL AT NIGHT. IS IT THE NIGHT-MARES AGAIN?

WHAT'S THE BIG DEAL WITH WHAT HE SAID?

FORGIVE ME. IT WAS A REFLEXIVE ACTION.

KEHO KEHO (COFF)

OH!

DO NOT SAY IT ALOUD, HARKAT!!

WH-WHAT'S WRONG, MR. CREPSLEY!?

WITCH?

WHATEVER YOU SAY WHILE WE ARE THERE...

...DO *NOT* CALL HER A WITCH.

...BUT I MUST MAKE ONE THING VERY CLEAR RIGHT NOW.

LISTEN CLOSELY. AS YOU KNOW, WE ARE HEADING FOR THE CAVE OF LADY EVANNA...

HEE!

HEE!

HEE!

BUT A WITCH?

LIKE, THAT KIND OF WITCH?

I THOUGHT SHE WAS AN INVENTOR OR SOMETHING.

KAKO

KAKO (BLIP)

SHE'S THE ONE WHO MADE THIS SELF-FOLDING POT, ISN'T SHE?

EVANNA IS CERTAIN TO HAVE USEFUL INFORMATION THAT WILL GUIDE US ON OUR SEARCH FOR THE VAMPANEZE LORD.

CHICHICHI (CHIRRUP)

YOU WILL UNDER-STAND WHEN YOU MEET HER.

MUCH OF HER TIME IS SPENT BREEDING FROGS.

SHE IS A WOMAN OF MANY TALENTS.

THIS IS GETTING EVEN STRANG-ER.

EXCUSE ME?

WHAT'S WRONG, DARREN?

SIGH...

HAVE YOU TOLD MR. CREPS-LEY?

MY BODY'S BEEN ITCHING ALL OVER FOR DAYS.

SFX: GARI (SCRATCH) GARI

NO. IT'S NOT THAT IMPORTANT, ANYWAY.

SFX: SUU (ZZZ) SUU

AND MY JOINTS ARE STRANGE-LY ACHY.

SFX: GUGU (RUB)

DON'T WORRY ABOUT ME. JUST... ENJOY YOUR REST.

SORRY ABOUT THIS. I'M ABOUT TO FALL ASLEEP.

SUU...

SUU...

WHAT ARE THESE PEOPLE GOING TO BE LIKE?

THE THIRD CHOSEN HUNTER...

LADY EVANNA, THE WOMAN WHO CANNOT BE CALLED A WITCH.

"UESS LL GO RAW SOME RESH ATER.

AL-READY EVE-NING.

AAAH!

OH GOOD. LOOKS LIKE HARKAT GOT HIS REST, AFTER ALL.

KUU (ZZZ)

MUKU (THUMP)

NO ITCHING, NO ACHES!

HMM...I FEEL REALLY GOOD TONIGHT FOR ONCE!

HERE WE GO...

ZA (THUD)

CHARNA'S GUTS!!

MOSHA (BRISTLE)

WHA—!

NOBODY HERE...

...

HARKAT!!

MR. CREPSLEY!!

BUT THIS IS...

...?

STOP WHO ARE YOU!!

BA (WHOOSH)

D... DARREN?

IT'S... ME!

...

YES! DON'T YOU RECOGNISE ME?

DON'T ATTAC

WE CALL THIS THE PURGE.

YOU'RE ALL HAIRY!

THIS RESULTS IN FULL-VAMPIRISM.

...ONE'S VAMPIRE CELLS EVENTUALLY ATTACK THE HUMAN CELLS AND CONVERT THEM.

IF ONE REMAINS A HALF-VAMPIRE FOR ROUGHLY FORTY YEARS...

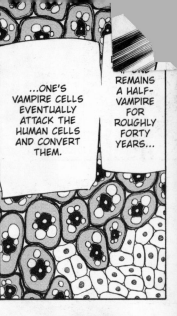

YOU MEAN I'VE BECOME A FULL-VAMPIRE?

PERHAPS THE VAMPIRE PRINCE BLOOD FROM THE CEREMONY SIX YEARS AGO SPED UP THE PROCESS.

THERE ARE MANY MORE CHANGES YET AHEAD OF YOU. THE NEXT FEW WEEKS WILL BE HARD!

YOU ARE NOT THAT LUCKY.

KOKI (CCRIK)

SHA (SAD)

SHA

I'M READY!

HERE WE GO.

YOO-HOO!

HMPH! HMPH!

...WERE THE INCREDIBLE SURGES OF ENERGY I EXPERIENCED...

DO DO DO DO (DMM)

GYUUUN (ZOOOM)

...AND THE WAYS I HAD TO BURN ALL OF IT OFF, JUST TO FALL ASLEEP.

THIS IS DRIVING ME CRAZY...

SFX: HAA (HUFF)

FINALLY, AFTER SIX WEEKS, THE TURMOIL CEASED.

IT LOOKS AS IF YOU ARE FINALLY SETTLING BACK INTO YOUR BODY.

NO DOUBT YOUR SENSES ARE RETURNING TO NORMAL AS WELL.

HMPH...

HE'S TALLER NOW.

GUGUGU (STRAIN)

SO, I'M STILL A HALF-VAMPIRE...

I DON'T KNOW WHETHER TO BE RELIEVED OR ANNOYED.

SOMETIME IN THE NEXT FEW YEARS, YOUR BLOOD *WILL* TURN COMPLETELY. THEN THERE IS NO TURNING BACK.

MOST IMPORTANTLY, YOU ARE STILL A HALF-VAMPIRE. THE TRANSFORMATION IS NOT COMPLETE.

ENJOY THE SUNLIGHT WHILE YOU STILL CAN. SOON YOU MUST BID IT FAREWELL FOREVER.

OH GREAT. I HAVE TO DO THIS AGAIN?

WHAT? I'M NOT A FULL-VAMPIRE?

I COULD PROBABLY USE A NEW PAIR OF SHOES AS WELL.

...THESE CLOTHES ARE GETTING A BIT SMALL.

SAY, MR. CREPSLEY...

HA HA HA.

カ
ラ
ン

カ
ラ
ン

KARAN

KARAN
(CLANK)

SALE

SALE

GU
(TUG)

GU

GU

I NEED THESE SUP- PLIES.

CAN I PAY FOR WHAT I JUST CHANGED INTO?

KARAN

KARAN (CLANK)

KARAN

YEAH, I DO ...

CHIRA (PEEK)

GOT A LICENSE?

JARA (CLINK)

JARA

WILL YOU BE NEEDING AMMO?

ER... YEAH...

IT LOOKS... GOOD.

YOUR OUTFIT SUITS YOU MUCH BETTER NOW, DARREN.

FISHY?

I SAW SOMEONE FISHY AT THE STORE.

HUMANS WHO KNOW THE TRUTH ABOUT VAMPIRE MARKS ARE UNCOMMON, BUT SOME EXIST.

HE MUST HAVE KNOWN WHAT THEY MEANT.

HE LOOK STARTLED WHEN HE SAW THE SCARS ON MY FINGER-TIPS.

NI
GRIND

IN THAT CASE, IT IS HIGHLY LIKELY...

AND LOTS OF THEM!

IT WAS GUNS!

AHA...

WHAT WAS HE BUYING THERE?

... THAT WE HAVE A VAMPIRE HUNTER ON OUR HANDS ...

...OR PERHAPS ONE OF THESE RUMORED VAMPETS.

...WE SHALL BE READY AND WAITING.

(IIN (SHING))

GOKU GUILD

WE WILL PROCEED AS PLANNED, BUT KEEP YOUR EYES OPEN.

SFX: ZA (ZSH) ZA

IF IT COMES TO THAT ...

WHAT IF AN ATTACK COMES?

TIME TO SEE WHAT THIS NEW PRINCE HAS GOT!

CHAPTER 59:
A DAYLIT BATTLE

YES, AND THEY MUST NUMBER THREE...NO, FOUR.

THEY'VE BEEN FOLLOWING US SINCE WE LEFT THAT LAST TOWN, HAVEN'T THEY?

THE RAYS WILL NOT HARM ME IN THE SHORT TIME IT WILL TAKE TO DEAL WITH THIS THREAT.

WILL YOU BE OKAY IN THE SUN?

WE WILL ACT AS THOUGH ALL IS NORMAL AND PRETEND TO SLEEP. WHEN THEY COME, WE WILL DEAL WITH THEM.

THEY WILL WAIT FOR FULL DAYLIGHT TO ATTACK.

WHAT'S THE PLAN? WHY ARE WE PREPARING... TO CAMP HERE?

AND I WILL PROTECT MY EYES, AS YOU DID DURING YOUR PURGE.

ALAS, I FIND IT HARD EVEN TO DISCARD JUNK.

CHA (CCHK)

I DIDN'T KNOW YOU STILL HAD THEM.

HEY, LOOK AT THAT! THE SUN-GLASSES I GAVE YOU FOR CHRISTMAS YEARS AGO!

YOU AND YOUR EXCUSES...

KA!
(FLASH)

GU! PA
(TWITCH)

SIX YEARS, IN FACT—SINCE THAT BATTLE WITH THE VAMPANEZE AT THE MOUNTAIN.

IT'S BEEN YEARS SINCE I'VE PREPARED TO FIGHT AN ENEMY TO THE DEATH.

JA
(CHK)

...HE'LL NEVER FIRE THE SECOND!

...I CAN MAKE SURE...

AS LONG AS I CAN AVOID THE FIRST BULLET...

...AND HARKAT AND I WILL EACH TAKE ANOTHER.

MR. CREPS-LEY WILL HANDLE TWO...

DON'T TENSE UP. THERE ARE FOUR OF THEM.

GASA
(SHFF)

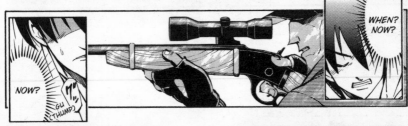

WHEN?
NOW?

NOW?

GU
(THUMP)

KACHIRI
(KCHIK)

KAKI
(CLICK)

NOW!!

DON

AH!

GASHAAA
(CLATTER)

MY BODY IS OVER-FLOWING WITH ENERGY AND POWER!

AMAZING! I MOVE MUCH FASTER THAN I'D EVER IMAGINED I COULD!

IT'S LIKE HE'S MOVING...

DIE, FILTHY VAMPIRE!

...IN SLOW MOTION!!

ZUBA (SLASH)

SIGH...

BURU (SHIVER)

BURU

NO, I'M MUCH MORE THAN THAT.

YOU'RE JUST... A KID...

AAAAHH!!

BOTO

BOTO (BLOP)

HEH-HEH-HEH...YOU SHOULD HAVE TAKEN MY OTHER HAND TOO!

THIS FIGHT IS JUST ABOUT OVER.

GOOD.

A HAND GRENADE!

DON'T MOVE!

EASY, EASY!

IF THIS GOES OFF, IT TAKES YOU WITH ME.

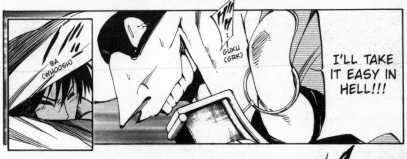

BA (WHOOSH)

GUKU (GRK)

I'LL TAKE IT EASY IN HELL!!!

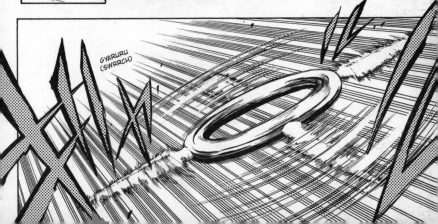

GYARURU (SWRRCH)

DOKA
(THUKK)

GURUN
(SHUFF)

WHO...
WHO ARE
YOU?

ONLY EVER
TURN YOUR
BACK ON A
CORPSE!

DIDN'T
VANEZ
BLANE
TEACH YOU
THAT?

KORO
(ROLL)

WHAT
KIND OF
WEAPON
IS THAT?
AND WHO
THREW
IT?

86

A VAMPET! I SHOULD HAVE KNOWN.

MISERABLE CURS!

ER, EXCUSE ME...

IT'S AN HONOUR TO MEET YOU, SIRE!

I'VE HEARD THE RUMORS.

PRINCE VANCHA MARCH, I PRESUME.

AND YOU MUST BE THE CUB PRINCE I HAVE HEARD SO MUCH ABOUT.

OF COURSE IT IS.

I'M ACTUALLY ON MY WAY TO LADY EVANNA'S TO FIND NEWS OF THIS VAMPANEZE LORD.

IT'S GOOD TO SEE YOU, LARTEN.

VANCHA! I THOUGHT YOU WERE FARTHER NORTH, SIRE!

ON THE BASIS OF THIS FIGHT, I HAVE TO SAY I'M NOT OVERLY IMPRESSED!

I FIGURED AS MUCH.

AH! AS ARE WE.

I'VE BEEN TRAILING YOU FOR THE LAST COUPLE OF NIGHTS.

I WANTED TO OBSERVE THIS NEW PRINCE FROM AFAR FOR A WHILE.

HE HAS POOR CONTROL OF HIS ABILITIES, AND HIS INEXPERIENCE IN BATTLE IS APPARENT AT FIRST GLANCE.

BACHII
(SMACK)

BWA-HA-HA-HA! NO USE GETTING STIFF ABOUT IT, YOUNG PRINCE!

BIRI
BIRI
(WINCE)

HUH!?

I ERRED, SIRE. YOU ARE CORRECT. I LET THE TEAM DOWN.

WELL, I CAN'T DENY HIS PERCEPTION.

NIYAA
(SMIRK)

I APOLOGIZE MOST HUMBLY.

BORI

BARI
(CHOMP)

BORI
(CHEW)

PERSONALLY, I'D SAY YOU PUT UP A DECENT FIGHT... FOR A HALF-VAMPIRE!

BUT EVERYTHING IN LIFE COMES DOWN TO ACCLIMATION, DOESN'T IT!?

HRMF! HMPH!

DOKKA
(THUD)

GASHI
(SWAP)

SO THIS IS THE LITTLE PERSON WHO TALKS.

HARKAT MULDS, ISN'T IT?

!!

HE'S BITING OFF HIS TOE-NAILS!

PU
(SPIT!)

...CHEW THEIR TOE-NAILS.

AND I DON'T TRUST VAMPIRES WHO...

I DON'T TRUST DESMOND TINY OR ANY OF HIS STUMPY DISCIPLES.

I MIGHT AS WELL TELL YOU STRAIGHT UP, MULDS.

BUHA (BFFT)

NIGO (SMIRCH)

SIRE.

I THINK WE'RE GOING TO GET ALONG FINE, MULDS!

WA HA HA HA HA

LOTS, AS A MATTER OF FACT.

ANY NEWS FROM VAMPIRE MOUN-TAIN?

I HAVEN'T MET WITH ANY GENERALS LATELY, LARTEN.

YES, I SEE...

AND I DON'T THINK IT TAKES A GENIUS TO SURMISE...

...THAT *I'M* THE THIRD HUNTER.

BUT THESE ARE DANGEROUS TIMES, VANCHA. THE FUTURE OF OUR RACE IS AT STAKE.

I JUST DON'T TRUST THAT EVIL MEDDLER, TINY!

I WOULD BE MOST SURPRISED IF YOU WERE NOT, SIRE.

SHE GUARDS HER TONGUE CLOSELY, BUT SHE SPEAKS THE TRUTH.

ALL THE MORE REASON FOR US TO SEEK OUT EVANNA'S CAVE.

YEAH...AT LEAST, I THINK SO.

GUGO (SNORT)

FUGO (SNRRT)

IS HE REALLY...A VAMPIRE PRINCE?

HE COULD RACE GAVNER TO SEE WHO SNOOZES FIRST.

HE'S ALREADY ASLEEP!

GOAA (SHNRR) *NGAA (NZZ)*

GORON (ROLL)

WAKE ME WHEN IT'S DUSK!

WELL, WE'LL SAVE IT FOR TONIGHT.

VANCHA CHOOSES TO LIVE ROUGHLY, BUT HE IS THE FINEST OF VAMPIRES.

DO NOT BE FOOLED BY APPEAR- ANCES.

GUUUU (ZZZZ)

SUPII (SWEE)

WELL, IF YOU SAY SO...

GOOO (SNORE)

GAAA (SNORR)

CHAPTER 60:
THE THIRD HUNTER

...WE CROSSED PATHS WITH PRINCE VANCHA MARCH, THE THIRD HUNTER.

ON OUR JOURNEY TO THE CAVE OF LADY EVANNA TO FIND CLUES ABOUT THE LORD OF THE VAMPANEZE...

...HUH? VANCHA?

MMM... MMM...

GABA (LURCH)

ENOUGH OF THE SNORING...

PIPE DOWN ALREADY!!

SFX: GOSHI (RUB) GOSHI

HEH HEH...

FUAAA (YAAAWN)

WHERE COULD HE HAVE GONE?

スー (ZZZ)

スー...

スー

SUU (ZZZ)

SUU...

SUU

ゴシゴシ

DIDN'T I TELL YOU TO WAKE ME UP WHEN THE SUN WENT DOWN?

GASA (RUSTLE)
GASA

THE SUN IS STILL HIGH IN THE SKY...

IT'S A BIT EARLY FOR THAT YET...

KA (FLASH)

 ...BUT ACCORDING TO ANCIENT LEGENDS...

NOW MOST HAVE FORGOTTEN ALL ABOUT THEM...

IF WE'RE SUPPOSED TO BE DESCENDED FROM WOLVES, WHY DOES IT KILL VAMPIRES?

 LOOK AT WOLVES. THEY CAN ENDURE THE SUN-LIGHT.

 WELL, NO, NOT EXACTLY...

 ...RESULTING IN THE CREATION OF VAMPIRES.

JUUU (FZZZ)

...MR. TINY EXPERIMENTED ON WOLVES AND MIXED THEIR BLOOD WITH THAT OF HUMANS...

 ...AND MADE US SLAVES OF THE NIGHT.

 THEY SAY HE WAS AFRAID WE'D GROW TOO POWERFUL...

PERHAPS. BUT IF THOSE LEGENDS ARE TRUE, OUR SUN-RELATED WEAKNESS IS ALSO TINY'S WORK.

 BUT THAT'S RIDICU-LOUS.

 WE HAVE TO TAKE ON THE ENEMY'S MANSERVANT, LOOK IT FULL IN ITS FACE, AND SPIT IN ITS EYE!!

NOTHING'S AS AWFUL AS SLAVERY, AND THERE'S ONLY ONE WAY TO WIN BACK OUR FREEDOM— *FIGHT!!*

QUITE SIMPLE, REALLY!

BUT HOW CAN YOU FIGHT THE SUN!?

YEP. THE SUN.

TINY'S MAN-SERVANT? YOU DON'T MEAN...?

...THEN I WIN !!!

I INTENTION-ALLY EXPOSE MYSELF TO ITS LIGHT, AND IF I CAN HANDLE IT WITHOUT DYING...

V-VANCHA !?

GET A GRIP!!

GAKU (SLUMP)

THAT'S WIN-NING?

BUT ALAS...

HA HA...

...I HAVE BEEN BESTED.

IT SEEMS THAT ONCE AGAIN ...

SFX: FURA (STAGGER)

CLEARLY I'VE A LONG WAY TO GO IN THIS BATTLE!

BROUGHT BACK TO CAMP BY A MERE STRAPLING!

I WON'T HAVE YOU GROVELLING TO ME.

IT'S "VANCHA," "MARCH," OR "HEY, UGLY!" WHILE WE'RE ON THE TRAIL.

NONE OF THAT "SIRE" BUSINESS, LARTEN!

YOU ARE STILL CONTINUING YOUR BATTLE WITH THE SUN, SIRE?

GA HA HA HA

VERY WELL... UGLY.

MY RECORD IS CLOSE TO EIGHTY MINUTES OF SUNLIGHT!

A HUNDRED YEARS!?

DARREN, MULDS, THAT GOES FOR YOU AS WELL!

BAN BAN (WHAM)

BUT I'M BADLY BURNED AT THE END, AND IT TAKES NEARLY A WEEK TO RECOVER!

... PROBABLY THE BEST PART OF A CENTURY.

WELL, I'M MORE THAN THREE HUNDRED NOW, SO...

HOW LONG HAS THIS WAR OF YOURS AGAINST THE SUN LASTED?

ZUZL (SNIFF)

HE EATS ONLY RAW MEAT AND VEGETABLES, AND DRINKS NOTHING BUT FRESH WATER, BLOOD, AND MILK.

VANCHA IS AN EXTREMELY PICKY VAMPIRE.

DON'T COOK IT, EVEN A BIT.

LEAVE THE MEAT AS IT IS.

THE ONE THING I CANNOT FATHOM, HOWEVER, IS THE REFUSAL TO SLEEP IN A COFFIN.

THERE ARE MANY THINGS WE CAN LEARN FROM VANCHA'S LIFESTYLE.

I INSIST ON LIVING EXACTLY AS THE VAMPIRES OF OLD DID—NO MORE, NO LESS!

URP...

...I'VE HUNTED!

GOT 'IM!

BECHOA (SPLORT)

?!!

BUUN! (BUZZ)

GABI (CHOMP)

GABU

SAME WITH THESE CLOTHES! THEY'RE SEWED TOGETHER FROM THE SKINS OF ANIMALS THAT...

PU... (PTOO)

イプ リ!!

SO LET'S SEE: HE CHEWS HIS TOENAILS, FIGHTS THE SUN EVERY DAY...

...AND HE'S SUPPOSED TO BE ABLE TO OVER-COME THE TERRIBLE VAMPANEZE LORD? HOW?

IS IT MUCH LONGER TO LADY EVANNA'S CAVE, LARTEN?

ONLY A FEW DAYS AT MOST, I SHOULD THINK.

NO THANK YOU, VANCHA. I DO NOT LOOK FORWARD TO THE BUSINESS END OF YOUR SHURIKENS.

THAT BATTLE AGAINST THE VAMPETS WAS GREAT. IT'S GOTTEN ME IN THE MOOD FOR A GOOD SPAR!

BY THE WAY, LARTEN!

WHAT IS SHE LIKE?

JUST WAIT UNTIL YOU SEE HER FACE!

...SHE'S BOTH THE FAIREST AND LEAST ATTRACTIVE OF ALL WOMEN!

IF I HAD TO PUT IT SIMPLY...

WANT ME TO SHOW YOU?

...I TAKE IT LITERALLY!

BAKI!

BAKI-(CRAK)

BUT WHEN IT COMES TO HAND-TO-HAND COMBAT...

NOPE. JUST THE SHURIKENS.

DON'T YOU USE ANYTHING ELSE, LIKE A KNIFE OR A...?

NIYA (SMIRK)

THEN HOW DO YOU FIGHT WITH SOMEONE WHO HAS A SWORD?

KNOW WHY?

ONE WHO LEARNS TO FIGHT WITH HIS HANDS ALWAYS HAS THE ADVANTAGE OVER THOSE WHO RELY ON SWORDS AND KNIVES.

I WAS THROWN ONTO MY BACK BEFORE I EVEN KNEW WHAT HAPPENED!

CAN YOU STAND, DAR-REN?

HYUN (SWISH)

HYUN

THEY USE THEM TO HIDE THAT FEAR.

IF YOU ASK ME, WEAPONS ARE TOOLS OF FEAR, USED BY THOSE WHO ARE AFRAID.

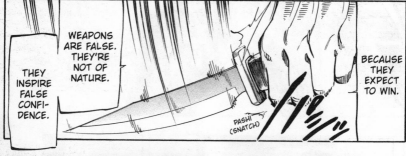

THEY INSPIRE FALSE CONFI-DENCE.

WEAPONS ARE FALSE. THEY'RE NOT OF NATURE.

BECAUSE THEY EXPECT TO WIN.

PASHI (SNATCH)

DEATH IS THE WORST THIS WORLD CAN THROW AT YOU, DARREN.

WHEN I FIGHT, I EXPECT TO DIE. EVEN NOW, WHEN I SPARRED WITH YOU...

IF YOU ACCEPT IT, IT HAS NO POWER OVER YOU.

...I ACCEPTED DEATH AND RESIGNED MYSELF TO IT.

SU
(SHH)

HERE'S YOUR KNIFE BACK.

STILL FEEL LIKE USING IT?

WELL, THERE'S NO NEED TO MAKE THE SWITCH *NOW!* YOU'VE GOT PLENTY OF TIME TO LEARN!

BAN (WHAM)

BAN

BWA-HA-HA-HA!!

ARE YOU SAYING YOU DON'T DESPISE THEIR KIND?

YOU THINK WE SHOULD LEARN FROM THE VAMPANEZE?

I THINK ALL VAMPIRES COULD STAND TO LEARN FROM THE VAMPANEZE THAT WAY.

BUT AT THE VERY LEAST, YOU SHOULD HAVE TASTE IN YOUR WEAPONS.

...BUT OTHERWISE I ADMIRE THEM.

I DON'T AGREE WITH THEIR FEEDING HABITS ...

VAMPANEZE ARE NOBLE AND TRUE.

BASA (FLAP)

JUST TAKE WHAT LESSONS FROM HIM YOU CAN.

DO NOT SPEND TOO MUCH TIME WORRYING ABOUT THINGS.

PON (PAT)

WHAT DID I TELL YOU? VANCHA IS A VAMPIRE AMONG VAMPIRES.

ANYTIME YOU WANT!

SURE!

WOULD YOU TEACH ME THE WAYS OF UNARMED COMBAT?

VANCHA!!

LOOK AT 'EM!

WOW!!

FROGS. THEY'RE ALERTING EVANNA THAT SHE HAS VISITORS.

WHAT'S MAKING ALL THAT NOISE?

GOE (CROAAK)

GGUE (GROKK)

IT'S DEATH IN THIRTY SECONDS.

THOSE FROGS HAVE POISON SACS ON THEIR TONGUES.

CAREFUL YOU DON'T STEP ON ANY.

BE CERTAIN *NOT* TO CALL HER A WITCH.

ONE LAST REMIND-ER.

WHAT!?

...THE CONSE-QUENCES COULD BE LETHAL!

SHE HAS A QUICK TEMPER, AND IF WE WERE TO RILE HER...

WHAT'S THIS?

ズ (STOMP)

ズッ

WH-WHAT DO YOU MEAN, LETHAL? YOU NEVER MENTIONED SHE...

VAMPIRES! ALWAYS UGLY, BLOODY VAMPIRES!

GOE

GUE

17

110

YOU MEAN THIS...

...IS LADY EVANNA!?

OH, YOU ARE SHAMELESS!

YOU'RE ONLY SAYING THAT TO PLEASE ME.

GABA (SQUISH)

BWA-HA-HA! AND YOU'RE UGLIER THAN EVER...

...LADY EVANNA!

CHAPTER 61:
LADY EVANNA

EVANNA
...

LAR-
TEN.

GA HA
HA HA

YOU'VE
PUT ON
SOME
WEIGHT,
SIRE.

MY
LITTLE
VANCHA
...

PASHI
(SWAK)

BYU
(WHOOSH)

DOSHIIN
(KATHWAMM)

BUCHI
(SMOOSH)

WISE BOY...

SHE DIDN'T JUST WIN, SHE DOMINATED HIM!

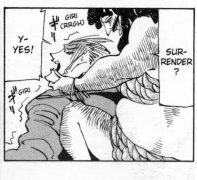

GIRI
(CRRGH)

Y-YES!

GIRI

SUR-RENDER?

YOU HAVE CHANGED IN MANY WAYS, WITHIN AND WITHOUT, BUT I RECOGNISE YOU.

YES, HARKAT. THIS IS NOT YOUR FIRST VISIT.

BEFORE !?

YOU, HARKAT, ARE WELCOME, AS YOU WERE BEFORE.

ALAS, NO. I CAN'T SAY. THAT'S FOR YOU TO FIND OUT.

WHO WAS I? CAN YOU... TELL ME?

YOU MEAN... YOU KNOW WHO I WAS... BEFORE I BECAME A LITTLE PERSON?

SFX: GEHO (COUGH) GEHO

HE WAS STRUCK BY THE PURGE AS WE TRAVELLED HERE.

I THOUGHT YOU WOULD BE YOUNGER.

SO THIS IS THE BOY PRINCE.

KUI (TUG)

MIND THE FROGS!

!!!

APPEARANCES, DARREN.

HA-HA-HA. WHAT DID I LOOK LIKE TO YOU JUST NOW?

NEVER LET THEM FOOL YOU...

AH, SO YOU *DO* REMEMBER.

EVANNA. THAT FORM...

I'M A SORCERESS. AN ENCHANTRESS. A CREATURE OF MANY MAGICAL TALENTS.

I AM NOT A *WITCH*.

SFX: BUN (SHAKE) BUN

THERE'S A STORY?

...HOW HE GOT THAT SCAR?

DID LARTEN EVER TELL YOU...

YOU MOST CERTAINLY WERE. HA-HA-HA...

I WAS YOUNG AND FOOLISH!

PLEASE, LADY, DO NOT SPEAK OF IT!

I ALWAYS WONDERED WHY YOU WERE SO COY ABOUT THAT! WE NORMALLY BOAST ABOUT OUR SCARS!

THAT'S HOW HE GOT IT?

LARTEN GOT TIPSY ON WINE AND TRIED TO KISS ME.

I WAS WEARING ONE OF MY BEAUTIFUL FACES.

YOU ARE CRUEL, EVANNA...

SO I GAVE HIM A LITTLE SCRATCH TO TEACH HIM SOME MANNERS.

IT IS FOR-GOTTEN, LADY.

THE SCAR IS PART OF ME NOW. I AM PROUD OF IT.

I FEEL GUILTY FOR LUMBERING YOU WITH THAT SCAR, LARTEN.

I SHOULDN'T HAVE CUT SO DEEPLY.

THERE IS NO NEED—

STILL, I HAVE PRESENTED YOU WITH GIFTS OVER THE YEARS, BUT THEY HAVEN'T SATISFIED ME.

PACHIN (SNAP)

...JUST A LITTLE... TOKEN.

I THINK AT LAST I HAVE A GIFT THAT WILL MAKE AMENDS. IT'S NOT SOMETHING YOU CAN TAKE...

SHUT UP AND LET ME FINISH!

GUE (CROAK)

GOE (GROKK)

?

MR. CREPSLEY HADN'T MOVED.

I THINK WE SHOULD LEAVE HIM ALONE FOR A WHILE.

COME INTO THE CAVE, YOU THREE.

THE FROGS STAYED, HELD THEIR SHAPE, AND KEPT MR. CREPSLEY COMPANY...

...AS HE GAZED SORROW-FULLY AT THE FACE OF HIS ONETIME MATE AND THOUGHT ABOUT THE PAINFUL PAST.

YOU MUST BE TIRED FROM YOUR LONG JOURNEY.

COME INSIDE AND EAT.

I PREFER YOU WHEN YOU'RE BEAUTIFUL.

I FEEL MORE COMFORTABLE THIS WAY.

WEREN'T EXPECTING ME TO TURN BACK?

!!

EAT UP, DEAR.

I AM A VEGETARIAN.

AND ARE YOU STILL ON THIS COW FOOD, LADY?

(SHAGU) (MUNCH)

YOU MIGHT SAY THAT.

SOUNDS GOOD...AS THOUGH YOU ALREADY KNOW WHAT'LL HAPPEN.

WHEN I RETURN, WE SHALL HAVE A LONG TALK ABOUT YOUR JOURNEY.

IF YOU WILL EXCUSE ME, I HAVE BUSINESS TO SEE TO.

BASA (FLAP)

EVANNA DOES INDEED BEAR A RELATION TO VAMPIRES.

THAT'S VERY PERCEPTIVE OF YOU.

GORO (GROLL)

SHE SEEMS MUCH LIKE A VAMPIRE... BUT NOT.

LADY EVANNA IS A VERY MYSTERIOUS PERSON.

NI (GRIND)

BUT I THOUGHT VAMPIRES COULDN'T BEAR CHILDREN THE NORMAL WAY...

SHE IS THE ONLY WOMAN IN THE ENTIRE WORLD WHO CAN GIVE BIRTH TO VAMPIRE CHILDREN.

WOULD YOU LIKE TO HEAR THE STORY OF HER PAST?

IT IS A LONG-TOLD VAMPIRE LEGEND ...

...CORZA'S QUEST CONTINUED, HIS SEARCH GROWING EVER MORE DESPERATE.

...AND SOUGHT THE CURE TO VAMPIRE STERILITY. EVEN AFTER SARFA'S DEATH...

THERE WAS A VAMPIRE COUPLE NAMED CORZA AND SARFA WHO WISHED FOR A CHILD...

IT BEGINS WELL OVER A THOUSAND YEARS AGO.

TINY TOOK SOME OF CORZA'S BLOOD AND MIXED IT WITH THAT OF A PREGNANT WOLF, WORKING STRANGE CHARMS ON HER.

EVENTUALLY, TINY RELENTED. HE SAID HE'D CREATE A WOMAN CAPABLE OF BEARING A VAMPIRE'S CHILD.

FOR TWO CENTURIES, CORZA PESTERED TINY AND BEGGED HIM TO GIVE THE VAMPIRES HOPE.

FINALLY, HIS TRAIL LED HIM TO THAT MEDDLER WITH THE WATCH, DESMOND TINY.

...OR DESTROY US COMPLETELY!

A BOY AND GIRL WHO WOULD EITHER MAKE THE CLAN MORE POWERFUL THAN EVER...

THAT WOLF GAVE BIRTH TO TWO HUMAN CHILDREN.

YES, EVANNA.

BUT THE GIRL WAS...?

NO ONE KNOWS IF THE BOY STILL LIVES...

WITHIN A YEAR, THE CHILDREN WERE ADULTS AND LEFT TO SEEK THEIR DESTINY IN THE WILDS.

HAVE YOU EVER ASKED EVANNA IF IT'S TRUE?

ONLY THREE PEOPLE KNOW THE TRUTH—DESMOND TINY, THE BOY, AND LADY EVANNA.

IS THE LEGEND TRUE?

I'VE ALWAYS PREFERRED A STIRRING GOOD LEGEND TO BORING OLD FACTS.

YOU KNOW WHAT, HARKAT?

I HATE TO INTERRUPT ALL THE FUN...

THAT'S THE KEY TO FIGHTING UNARMED!

LEARN TO ANTICIPATE YOUR OPPONENT'S NEXT MOVE!

THAT'S IT! MUC BETTER

...BUT I HAVE RE- TURNED.

AND NOW WE SHALL DISCUSS OUR BUSINESS HERE.

THE THREE HUNTERS OF THE VAMPANEZE LORD...

I AM FAMILIAR WITH THE DETAILS OF YOUR STORY.

I LACK DESMOND'S CLEAR INSIGHT INTO THE FUTURE, BUT I SEE SOME OF WHAT IS TO COME, OR MIGHT COME.

YOU... HAVE?

I HAVE BEEN WAITING FOR YOU FOR MANY CENTURIES.

I DOUBT IF EVEN DESMOND KNOWS THAT.

DO YOU KNOW IF WE'LL BE SUCCESSFUL?

IN THIS CASE, CHANCE DECIDES WHICH PATH THE WORLD WILL TAKE.

...EACH POSSIBILITY AS STRONG AS THE OTHER.

TWO POSSIBLE FUTURES LIE AHEAD OF YOU...

NO, I WON'T.

BUT YOU WON'T TELL US, WILL YOU?

YES, OF COURSE.

HAVE YOU ANY IDEA WHERE HE IS!?

WHAT ABOUT THE LORD OF THE VAMPANEZE?

YOU MUST SEARCH FOR HIM YOUR- SELVES.

IF I TOLD, I WOULD CHANGE THE COURSE OF THE FUTURE, AND THAT'S NOT ALLOWED.

WILL YOU TELL US HOW WE SHOULD FIND HIM, AND WHEN?

THEN WHY COME WITH US NOW?

HOWEVER, I'LL PLAY NO PART IN THE QUEST TO FIND THE VAMPANEZE LORD.

I WILL ACCOMPANY YOU ON THE NEXT LEG OF YOUR JOURNEY.

MY REASONS WILL BECOME CLEAR IN TIME.

THERE'S SOMEONE I WISH TO MEET. I COULD SEEK HIM ALONE, BUT I PREFER NOT TO.

MAKE YOUR PREPARA- TIONS.

BASA
(FLAP)

SHUBABABABA (ZWOOOSH)

BASA (FLUMP)

BASHI (THUMP)

DOSA (THUD)

NOW IS AS GOOD A TIME AS EVER!

IF THAT'S SETTLED, I'LL PACK MY THINGS AND WE'LL TAKE TO THE ROAD.

...PLAYING MIND GAMES, NO DOUBT.

...DESMOND SHOULD HAVE TOLD YOU THIS, BUT HE OBVIOUSLY CHOSE NOT TO...

ONE MORE THING...

PITA (STOP)

FOUR TIMES YOUR PATHS WILL CROSS WITH THAT OF THE VAMPANEZE LORD. IF YOU FAIL, THE VAMPANEZE ARE DESTINED TO WIN.

IT IS TO PREPARE YOU, SHOULD MATTERS COME TO THE WORST.

I TELL YOU THE FOLLOWING NOT TO FRIGHTEN YOU, BUT BECAUSE I THINK YOU SHOULD KNOW.

...

MEAN-ING...?

...TO WITNESS THE FALL OF THE VAMPIRE CLAN.

...ONLY ONE OF YOU WILL BE ALIVE...

IF YOU HAVE FACED THE VAMPANEZE LORD FOUR TIMES AND FAILED TO KILL HIM...

THE
OTHER
TWO...

...WILL BE
DEAD.

...THEN ONLY ONE OF THE THREE OF YOU WILL LIVE TO SEE THE FALL OF THE VAMPIRE CLAN...

IF YOU HAVE FAILED FOUR TIMES TO KILL THE VAMPANEZE LORD...

CHAPTER 62:
CIRQUE DU FREAK

ON THE SECOND DAY SINCE LEAVING EVANNA'S CAVE WITH HER IN TOW, WHEN WE MADE CAMP...

IT WAS A JOURNEY WITHOUT A DESTINATION.

LADY EVANNA REFUSED TO TELL US ANYTHING ABOUT THE LORD OF THE VAMPANEZE'S WHEREABOUTS.

HE WON'T SAY IT, BUT I THINK HE'S WORRIED ABOUT EVANNA'S PROPHECY.

VANCHA'S BEEN QUIET FOR THE PAST DAY.

BUT WHEN IT'S STATED SO PLAINLY...

IT'S A BATTLE FOR THE FATE OF OUR PEOPLE. DEATH WAS BOUND TO BE A PART OF IT.

UH...
UH...

......

HE HAS THESE NIGHTMARES AT TIMES! WE NEED TO WAKE HIM UP!

AAH!

WHAT'S WRONG WITH HIM!?

AAHH!!

HOLD!!

HARKAT!!

AAHH!!

AAHH!!!!

!!!!!

...WHO HARKAT WAS IN HIS PREVIOUS LIFE?

DID DESMOND SAY NOTHING ABOUT REVEALING...

YOU CAN READ THEM?

HAA (CHUFF)

HAA

GUU (PRESS)

A A H

BAD DREAMS...

DRAGONS...

BUT ONE WHO SPEAKS THE LANGUAGE OF THE DRAGONS COULD HELP.

NO, HE MUST LEARN THE TRUTH HIMSELF.

IF YOU TOLD HIM WHO HE WAS, WOULD THAT EASE HIS NIGHTMARES?

NOBLE... BUT FOOLISH.

YES, BUT HARKAT CHOSE TO COME WITH US, TO SEARCH FOR THE VAMPANEZE LORD.

AAAH!
RRGH!

I'VE NEVER EVEN SEEN A DRAGON! I THOUGHT THEY WERE IMAGINARY!

ME!!?

IN FACT, *YOU* COULD HELP, DARREN.

GOOD CHILD.

TELL ME WHAT I HAVE TO DO.

WILL YOU HELP, OR WON'T YOU?

OKAY.

I WILL GUIDE YOU THE REST OF THE WAY.

LAY YOUR HANDS ON HARKAT'S HEAD, CLOSE YOUR EYES, AND FOCUS.

GO (WHOOSH)

ARE YOU READY?

INTO HARKAT'S NIGHT-MARES WE GO ...

132

IT WAS JUST A PART OF HARKAT'S NIGHTMARE, NOTHING MORE.

I'M BACK...

YES...

HARKAT WILL NOT HAVE THE NIGHT-MARES FOR A TIME.

YOU DID WELL.

A A A A H!!

JITO (DRIP)

SUU

SUU (ZZZ)

GASHI (GRAB)

AND TO THINK, WE'VE BEEN MOPING AROUND, AFRAID OF DEATH LIKE A BUNCH OF IDIOTS!

HEH-HEH... THE LITTLE RUNT'S BEEN CARRYING A HEAVY BURDEN ON HIS SHOULDERS ALL THIS TIME.

WHAT WOULD A VAMPIRE DO, DARREN?

WE MUST CHOOSE A DESTINATION FOR NOW.

HOWEVER, IT DOES US NO GOOD TO SEARCH FOR THIS VAMPANEZE LORD BLINDLY AND WITHOUT PURPOSE.

WOULDN'T YOU?

I'D RATHER DIE BEFORE-HAND, FIGHTING FOR OUR FUTURE!!

IF BY SOME CHANCE WE FAIL FOUR TIMES, I'M NOT GOING TO BE THE ONE ALIVE, WATCHING THE WALLS OF OUR WORLD COME CRASHING DOWN.

SOUNDS LIKE YOU'VE GOT A PLACE IN MIND ALREADY.

FOLLOW HIS HEART!

BRAVE WORDS, BUT TRUE.

WE WILL GO TO THE CIRQUE DU FREAK !!!

I'D LIKE TO SEE HOW EVRA'S DOING.

EVRA...

WHICH MEANS WE HAVE BUT ONE DESTINATION.

AND I, MY GOOD FRIEND, MR. TALL.

WE'VE BEEN TOO FOCUSED ON FATE AND PROPHECIES. WE NEED TO CONCENTRATE ON ALL WE CAN ACTUALLY DO...

GUGOO GIZZZZ

GAA GIZZ

VANCHA'S RIGHT. THERE'S NO USE FRETTING OVER A FUTURE THAT'S STILL A MYSTERY TO US.

YES. HE WAS TERRIBLE.

YOU SAW THE SHADOWY MAN?

WHAT I SAY NOW IS BETWEEN YOU AND ME. IT MUST GO NO FARTHER.

THERE IS MORE THAT YOU MUST KNOW ABOUT THE NIGHTMARE HARKAT WAS HAVING.

IT'S BEEN SIX YEARS.

EVRA...

I COULDN'T MAKE OUT HIS FACE, BUT I FELT I KNEW HIM.

BUT THERE WAS SOMETHING FAMILIAR ABOUT HIM.

PIKU (TWITCH)

SURE, LADY EVANNA.

MAY WE SPEAK, DARREN?

THE FUTURE?

WHAT YOU SAW WAS A SHADE OF THE FUTURE, WHEN EITHER THE VAMPIRES OR THE VAMPANEZE HAVE TRIUMPHED.

THE WOULD-BE RULER OF THE ETERNAL NIGHT.

HE IS THE MASTER OF SHADOWS.

SO YOU SHOULD.

...BUT HE WILL, EVENTUALLY.

THE LORD OF THE SHADOWS HAS NOT YET COME INTO HIS OWN...

AND IN THE OTHER?

IN ONE, THE VAMPANEZE LORD HAS BECOME THE MASTER OF SHADOWS AND RULER OF THE DARK.

THE FUTURE HAS TWO PATHS, AND BOTH ARE WINDING AND TROUBLED.

...THE LORD OF THE SHADOWS IS YOU.

IN THE OTHER...

DAR-REN !!

EVRA !!

YOU MUST BE JOKING...

LET M INTRO DUCE THE FAMILY

AND MY FIRSTBORN, SHANCUS, IS NOW FIVE.

HE WAS NAMED AFTER YOU, DARREN!

URCHA IS THE MIDDLE CHILD, THREE YEARS OLD.

LILIA'S THE YOUNGEST AT TWO.

MY WIFE, MERLA. SHE CAN DETACH HER EARS AND USE THEM AS MINI-BOOMERANGS.

WAS THAT SAR-CASM?

HEY, YOU'RE ALL GROWN UP TOO.

THIS IS WILD... YOU'RE MARRIED AND YOU HAVE KIDS, EVRA!

YOU TURNED SHAN INTO SHANCUS! I LIKE IT!

I CAN'T BELIEVE YOU REMEMBER THAT!

WAS MERLA THE GIRL YOU NEEDED HELP PICKING OUT A PRESENT FOR?

HI EVERY-ONE!

DARREN, LARTEN! YOU'RE BACK!

THANKS!

YOU ARE WELCOME AT THE CIRQUE DU FREAK, SIRE VANCHA MARCH.

YOU KNEW... MY NAME...

WEL-COME, HARKAT.

HIBER-NIUS.

WELCOME BACK, LARTEN, DARREN.

HUH?

WAIT... "HAR-KAT" !?

LEFTY CAN TALK !?

YOU ARE HUNGRY?

I MADE SAUSAGES!

LADY EVANNA.

HIBERNIUS.

THEY KNOW EACH OTHER...

DARREN!

I NOT GOOD AT LANGUAGE. BUT EVRA IS PATIENT AND I SLOWLY LEARNING...

YOU CAN SPEAK ENGLISH NOW!

TRUSKA!!

SFX: HAFU (HUFF) HAFU

THEY KNOW EACH OTHER?

IT'S A SMALL WORLD...

NAUGHTY VANCHA!

BUT YOU'RE STILL AS GORGEOUS AS YOU'VE EVER BEEN!

I ALMOST DIDN'T RECOGNISE YOU, DARREN!

ARE YOU GOING TO DO YOUR ACT AGAIN, LARTEN?

... WE'VE GOT PLENTY OF PROBLEMS, BUT I FEEL A BIT POSITIVE FOR ONCE.

BETWEEN THE LORD OF THE VAMPANEZE AND THE MASTER OF SHADOWS...

IT'S A WONDERFUL THING TO HAVE A PLACE YOU CAN CALL A HOME OF SORTS.

I'M GLAD WE DECIDED TO COME BACK TO THE CIRQUE DU FREAK.

WE CANNOT TAKE SIDES, HIBERNIUS. WE HAVE NEITHER ALLIES NOR FOES.

I WISH YOU WOULD NOT DO THIS, EVANNA.

LADY EVANNA?

WHY IS SHE TAKING OFF ON HER OWN?

AND DRESSED THAT WAY...

 GOKU (GULP)

HOW FAR IS SHE GOING TO TRAVEL?

WE'VE GONE ABOUT TWO OR THREE MILES FROM CAMP.

BUT I CAN'T HELP BUT BE CURIOUS ABOUT THEIR CONVERSATION. WHAT DID SHE MEAN, "WE HAVE NEITHER ALLIES NOR FOES"?

IT'S INCREDIBLY RUDE OF ME TO FOLLOW HER LIKE THIS.

SHE'S ONLY WALKING, BUT HER SPEED IS ASTONISHING!

I HAVE A BAD FEELING ABOUT THIS!

I'LL LOSE SIGHT OF HER IF I DON'T FOCUS!

WAS THAT A SIGNAL?

A WHIS-TLE.

THERE'S SOME-ONE OUT THERE...

!?!?

HUFF

HUFF

WH-WHAT DOES THIS MEAN...?

WHY IS LADY EVANNA MEETING WITH... VAMPANEZE !?

WHAT IS EVANNA DOING WITH THE VAMPANEZE !?

CHAPTER 63: A SUSPICIOUS CONVERSATION

I HAVE TO LET MR. CREPSLEY AND VANCHA KNOW ABOUT THIS!

WE'RE NEVER SAFE! DON'T MAKE SUCH A MISTAKE AGAIN!

DAN (STOMP)

SORRY! I THOUGHT WE WERE SAFE WITH LADY EVANNA...

PUT THAT OUT, FOOL!

ANOTHER WHO LOOKED LIKE A SERVANT, AND ONE WITH PALE SKIN... PERHAPS A VAMPET?

ZUSA (SCRAPE)

IN THAT BRIEF MOMENT, I SAW SIX VAMPANEZE.

FOR THE FIRST TIME IN AGES...

HA HA HA...

I CAN NO LONGER WAIT... HERE I COME, MY DEAR...

IT IS EARLIER THAN I WOULD LIKE, BUT IT MUST BE SO.

HE HAS EVERY LAST PREPARATION MADE...

WELL DONE, HIBERNIUS!

THIS IS IMPORTANT! LISTEN TO ME!

WH-WHY THE SHOUTING, DARREN?

BIKU BIKU (TWITCH)

MR. CREPS-LEY!!!

CAN IT WAIT UNTIL TOMORROW? I HAVE AN URGENT APPOINTMENT WITH THIS COFFIN...

LARTEN!

I WILL SUMMON VANCHA AND HARKAT.

VERY WELL.

ARE YOU SUGGESTING THAT DARREN WAS MERELY SEEING THINGS? WELL?

I DOUBT THAT, ESPECIALLY OF EVANNA.

THE WITCH IS SELLING US OUT TO THE VAMPANEZE AS WE SPEAK!

DAN (SLAM)

DON'T FORGET, WE'RE AT WAR! THE LORD OF THE VAMPANEZE ISN'T THE ONLY THING WE HAVE TO WORRY ABOUT!

WOULD YOU TWO GET A GRIP?

I STILL CAN'T FULLY BELIEVE IT MYSELF. I CAN'T IMAGINE EVANNA BETRAYING US THAT WAY...

...BUT I KNOW MY DUTY.

I DON'T FANCY OUR CHANCES AGAINST HER...

AND WHAT IF EVANNA TAKES THEIR SIDE AGAINST US?

...WHICH MAKES A SURPRISE ATTACK OUR ONLY VIABLE OPTION!

IT'S KILL OR BE KILLED! WITH EVANNA, THAT MAKES NINE OF THEM...

I DOUBT IT'S COINCIDENCE THAT WE'RE HERE AT THE SAME TIME AS THEM.

WHAT DO YOU SAY, DARREN?

I THINK WE SHOULD FIGHT.

OF COURSE. HERE.

HEY... WATER.

BUT IF THIS IS FATE LEADING US STRAIGHT TO THE LORD OF THE VAMPANEZE...

...THEN WE'VE GOT NO CHOICE!

I DON'T LIKE IT...YET ANOTHER BATTLE TO THE DEATH.

SHURURURURU (SHWURRR)

VANCHA'S SHURIKEN MARKS...

AS LONG AS WE DISORIENT THEM BY AMBUSHING FROM ALL DIRECTIONS, WE'LL HAVE THE UPPER HAND!

THERE ARE NINE OF THEM, INCLUDING EVANNA... MORE THAN TWICE OUR NUMBER!

...THE START OF BATTLE!

GYAAAAH!

ZA
(ZSHH)

THERE SHOULD BE JUST TWO VAMPANEZE LEFT!

WE'VE TAKEN DOWN FOUR, AND MR. CREPSLEY AND VANCHA ARE EACH HANDLING ANOTHER NOW.

THE AMBUSH WAS A SUCCESS!

ARE YOU GOING TO STAND BY AND WATCH AS YOUR COMPANIONS ARE SLAUGHTERED?

THE TIP OF HIS BLADE IS A BLUR...

RGH!!

DAAN
(WHAAM)

EVEN IN DEATH MAY YOU BE TRIUMPHANT...

THEN I WILL NOT RAISE A HAND TO YOU.

...I WILL NOT.

WILL YOU RAISE YOUR BLADES TO **ME** TOO, LARTEN?

FAR MORE POWERFUL AND DANGEROUS THAN ANY VAMPANEZE I'VE SEEN BEFORE!

HE'S MIGHTY!!

BOTO (PLOP)

DIE...

SU (SSK)

OVER HERE! TWO ARE GETTING AWAY!!

BIKU (TWITCH)

CHARNA'S GUTS...

ZU (ZLRRSH)

ZU

NO, YOU...

THEY'RE ABOUT TO GET AWAY!

IF ONLY I WASN'T INJURED!

BA (ZIP)

AS LONG AS WE STOP THEM BEFORE THEY CAN FLIT!

160

KACHI
(CHK!K)

!?

BURU
(SHIVER)

GU
(CHMPH)

WHAT ARE YOU DOING, VANCHA!? YOU'RE LETTING HIM ESCAPE!

GA GANN ...
...

WHAT IS THE MEANING OF THIS ...?

WHY? WHY DID YOU LET THEM ESCAPE!?

NO...

...WAS MY BROTHER, GANNEN HARST.

AYE. THAT VAMPANEZE WHO JUST ESCAPED...

IS THIS TRUE, VANCHA...?

WE DID EVERYTHING TOGETHER...

WE WERE VERY CLOSE GROWING UP.

...INCLUDING JOINING THE VAMPANEZE...

CHAPTER 64: VANCHA'S PAST

YOU MEAN YOU'RE...

WHA—? VAM-PANEZE?

CHAPTER 64:
VANCHA'S PAST

I COULDN'T ACCUSTOM MYSELF TO THE KILLING.

BUT SOMETHING BEGAN TO EAT AWAY AT MY CONVICTIONS.

GANNEN AND I WERE BLOODED AS HALF-VAMPANEZE, AND SERVED TOGETHER FOR A FEW YEARS AS ASSISTANTS.

IT SICKENED ME, SO I DECIDED TO QUIT.

I WAS SENTENCED TO DEATH.

PRECISELY. NO VAMPANEZE WILL KILL ONE OF HIS OWN, BUT THAT LAW DOESN'T APPLY TO A HALF-VAMPANEZE.

I DIDN'T THINK IT WOULD BE THAT EASY TO LEAVE THE VAMPANEZE...

I WAS WARNED TO AVOID GANNEN AND ALL VAMPANEZE IN THE FUTURE. I NEVER SAW MY BROTHER AGAIN...

...UNTIL TONIGHT.

THE ONLY REASON I AM ALIVE TODAY IS BECAUSE OF GANNEN'S ASSISTANCE.

BUT GANNEN PLEADED FOR MY LIFE.

IN THE END I MADE UP MY MIND NOT TO FEED AT ALL, AND DIE.

I HAD NO WAY TO FEED ON MY VICTIMS WITHOUT DRINKING ENOUGH BLOOD TO KILL.

FOR SEVERAL YEARS I LIVED MISERABLY.

 BUT HOW CAN YOU BLOOD SOMEONE AS A VAMPIRE IF HE'S ALREADY BEEN BLOODED AS A VAMPANEZE?

 PARIS... BLOODED YOU?

 IT WAS THEN THAT I MET PARIS SKYLE.

A HALF-VAMPIRE CAN BECOME A VAMPANEZE, AND VICE VERSA.

 ...AND HE BLOODED ME ANYWAY.

 YES, LARTEN. PARIS KNEW THE RISKS...

...AND IN TIME TRAINED TO BE A GENERAL.

I WAS ABLE TO CONTROL MY FEEDING URGES NOW. I STUDIED UNDER PARIS...

AT THE SAME TIME, HE GAVE ME HIS VAMPIRE BLOOD, MAKING ME ONE OF YOUR KIND.

PARIS TOOK MY TAINTED BLOOD, AND HIS BODY'S NATURAL DEFENSES BROKE IT DOWN AND RENDERED IT HARMLESS.

SFX: GARI (SQUEEZE)

 AFTER I'D PROVEN MYSELF MANY TIMES, I WAS ALLOWED TO BE PROMOTED TO PRINCE.

BUT THIS COULD EASILY HAVE KILLED HIM, JUST AS IT COULD HAVE KILLED ME.

CASA
RUSTLE

CASA

PARIS KEPT MY PAST SECRET FROM EVERYONE EXCEPT THE OTHER PRINCES.

BURU
(SHIVER)

BURU

I'VE BEEN TER-RIFIED OF THIS...

...OF THE POSSIBILITY OF MY LOYALTIES BEING DIVIDED IF I MET GANNEN AGAIN, AS THEY HAVE BEEN TONIGHT.

THOUGHT YOU MIGHT LIKE IT BACK.

FEE! FI! FO! *THUMB!* I FOUND THIS.

ALL THE PAIN FROM MY THUMB IS FINALLY RUSHING BACK!

ZUKU

ZUKU
(THROB)

ISN'T THAT RIGHT?

YOU SHOULD HAVE BEEN A SPY, DARREN.

SNOOPS DON'T DESERVE SPECIAL FAVOURS.

I CAN DO IT... BUT I WON'T.

POSSIBLY.

CAN W STITCH IT BAC ON?

HIRA (SWISH)

HIRA

YES?

EVA NA ...

WELL...

YEAH...

... WAS IT GANNEN?

DARREN! YOUR THUMB ...

LET ME SEE IT.

BU!! (GOSO CRUSTLE)

I'M SORRY.

I WAS TOO WEAK TO STOP HIM.

DON'T APOLOGIZE.

170

NNG!

グ
″GU
(TUG)

THAT'S RIGHT. LOOK ON THE BRIGHT SIDE.

...AND YOU WILL HAVE TO MAKE DO WITHOUT.

THIS IS THE BEST WE CAN DO. IF IT GETS INFECTED, WE WILL CHOP IT OFF AGAIN...

IT IS UNFORTUNATE, BUT WE HAVE NOT BEEN HARMED BY YOUR SLIP, AND...

NONSENSE! ANY MAN WHO WOULD STRIKE A BROTHER IS NO MAN AT ALL.

I DON'T DESERVE TO LIVE.

IT'S MY *HEAD* YOU SHOULD BE CHOPPING OFF.

HA!
HA
HA
HA
HA

I TAKE NOBODY'S SIDE...

I WANT TO KNOW WHY SHE WAS CONSORTING WITH THE ENEMY AND PRETENDING TO BE AN ALLY!

NEVER MIND WHY SHE'S LAUGHING!

OH, LARTEN, IF ONLY YOU KNEW!

DID I SAY SOMETHING FUNNY?

AHA HA HA!

I LOOK UPON YOU AS SILLY, WARRING BOYS.

THE DIVIDE BETWEEN VAMPIRES AND VAMPANEZE IS OF NO INTEREST TO ME.

THE WAR OF THE SCARS?

I'VE SAT WITH THE HUNTERS AND STUDIED THEM.

NOW I'VE DONE LIKEWISE WITH THE HUNTED. IT'S GOOD TO KNOW IN ADVANCE THE QUALITY OF THOSE TO WHOM YOUR FUTURE IS TIED.

HOWEVER, I CANNOT SIT IDLY AS IT ALL HAPPENS.

WHICHEVER WAY THE WAR OF THE SCARS GOES, I'LL HAVE TO DEAL WITH THE VICTORS.

WH-WHAT IS IT, HARKAT?

OH!

IF YOU DID, YOU'D KNOW WHAT'S GOING ON.

KU CHEH

KU

KU

DO YOU FINE GENTLE-MEN READ MYSTERY NOVELS?

IF YOU HAVE SOME-THING THAT IS PRECIOUS, WHERE IS THE BEST PLACE TO HIDE IT?

HERE'S A LITTLE HINT.

WHAT?

...HE WAS NO SERVANT!!

THE MAN IN THE ROBES...NOT GANNEN...

PRECISELY. BY DRESSING HIM AND TREATING HIM AS A SERVANT, AS THEY HAVE DONE SINCE THEY TOOK THE ROAD...

...THE VAMPANEZE KNEW HE'D BE THE LAST TARGET ANY-ONE WOULD FOCUS ON IN THE EVENT OF AN ATTACK.

THAT SEEMINGLY INSIGNIFICANT SERVANT WAS THE LORD OF THE VAMPANEZE.

KOKI (CRIK)

THE FIRST OF YOUR PROMISED FOUR CHANCES TO KILL HIM HAS NOW PASSED...

...THE FAKE SERVANT, THE LORD OF THE VAMPANEZE.

GAKU (SLUMP)

HE FLED TO SAVE THE LIFE OF THE MAN HE WAS PROTECTING...

YOUR BROTHER DIDN'T RUN BECAUSE HE WAS AFRAID, VANCHA.

DAMN IT ALL!

DARREN...

GAYA

GAYA (MURMUR)

WHAT ARE YOU DOING, VANCHA!?

GET DOWN FROM THERE!

THAT SOUNDS LIKE TRUSKA...

TURN ME INTO ASH! ROAST ME! I DON'T CARE!!

BURN ME ALIVE! DO YOUR WORST!! SEE IF I GIVE A—

IT IS VANCHA!

TRUSKA, EVRA! WHAT'S GOING ON?

BECAUSE I SPARED THE LIFE OF MY BROTHER, OUR GREATEST ENEMY HAS ESCAPED AND OUR PEOPLE FACE DEFEAT.

AYE...BUT THIS IS A MAD WORLD, LARTEN.

COME DOWN, SIRE! THIS IS MADNESS!

GRR...

BETTER I PASS WITH IT THAN LINGER AND SHAME US ALL...

MY CHANCE TO KILL THE LORD OF THE VAMPANEZE HAS PASSED.

IT WON'T HELP, BUT IT WILL PUNISH...AND I DESERVE TO BE PUNISHED.

I SHOULD KNOW! I'VE DONE IT!

DYING WILL NOT HELP, VANCHA!!

I'M IN THE MOOD TO CRACK A FEW SKULLS BEFORE I DIE!

TAKE HEED, DARREN SHAN!

TA (TOKKO)

FF!!

BA (BOING)

BA (BOING)

DAR-REN!

AFTER ALL THE HAUGHTY LESSONS AND BOASTS, YOU'RE NOTHING BUT A COWARD AND A FOOL.

WHAT...?

VII... PIKU (TWITCH)

WHO GAVE YOU THE RIGHT TO QUIT!?

WHAT MAKES YOU THINK YOU CAN ABANDON THE QUEST AND DAMN US ALL!?

...I...I FAILED...

B- BUT...

WE HAVE LEARNED VALUABLE INFORMATION ABOUT THE ENEMY THIS TIME, WITHOUT LOSING ANY OF OUR OWN PEOPLE!

THERE ARE STILL THREE CHANCES REMAIN- ING!

BECAUSE HIS DUTY TO LEAD THE CLAN OUTWEIGHS EVERYTHING ELSE!

AND WHY IS IT THAT A PRINCE IS NOT EX- ECUTED IF HE FAILS A TRIAL?

...WOULD CONSIDER HOW TO REGAIN HIS HONOUR BY CAPITALIZING ON HIS REMAINING OPPORTUNITIES RATHER THAN FACE PUNISHMENT!

THE PROUD AND MIGHTY PRINCE VANCHA MARCH THAT I KNOW...

YOU'RE RIGHT, DARREN.

YEAH...

...AMONG OTHER THINGS I HAVE TO LEARN FROM YOU.

NOT TO MENTION YOUR LESSONS IN HAND-TO-HAND COMBAT...

OOO (RAHHH)

I'VE BEEN AN IDIOT, HAVEN'T I?

HAH!

THE BOY MAY MAKE A PRINCE YET.

...BY DARREN, NO LESS.

PRINCE VANCHA BEING BROUGHT TO HIS SENSES...

WE DECIDED IT WOULD BE FOR THE BEST IF WE LEFT THE CIRQUE DU FREAK.

WE DIDN'T WANT TO BRING THE ANGER OF OUR FOES ON THE CIRCUS FOLK.

THERE WAS STILL THE CHANCE THAT GANNEN AND HIS LORD WOULD RETURN FOR VENGEANCE.

SHE TOLD US SHE WAS RETURNING TO HER CAVE TO PREPARE FOR THE TRAGEDIES TO COME.

AFTER YESTERDAY'S ENCOUNTER, THE PATH OF FATE HAD FORKED YET AGAIN.

WE ALSO BADE FARE-WELL TO EVANNA.

DON'T YOU GO TAKING DOWN THAT VAMPANEZE LORD WITHOUT ME!

VANCHA AGREED TO RETURN TO VAMPIRE MOUNTAIN WITH THE NEWS OF OUR MEETING WITH THE ENEMY.

GAYA

GAYA (MURMUR)

EVRA, TRUSKA... I'M SORRY.

YOU HAVE TO LEAVE ALREADY? I WAS HOPING YOU'D STICK AROUND TO SEE THE SHOW...

YEAH, SHANCUS. I PROMISE!

WILL WE GET TO SEE YOU AGAIN?

H" GU (THG)

YOU TOO, LARTEN.

TAKE CARE, HIBERNIUS.

KILL HARST, AND YOU CAN INFLUENCE THE ODDS OF FUTURE SUCCESS TO WEIGH ON YOUR SIDE.

THE SIX YOU KILLED WERE NORMAL GUARDS WHO CAN BE REPLACED. HARST IS THE KEY.

ONLY MR. TINY CAN MEDDLE DIRECTLY.

I AM SORRY. I'D HAVE WARNED YOU, BUT THOSE WITH INSIGHT INTO THE FUTURE ARE FORBIDDEN TO CHANGE IT.

...IS THE PRIME PROTECTOR OF THE LORD OF THE VAMPANEZE.

WHAT I *CAN* TELL YOU IS THAT GANNEN HARST...

THERE WILL ALWAYS BE A HOME FOR YOU HERE AT THE CIRQUE DU FREAK!

RETURN ANYTIME YOU WISH!

BACK WHERE WE STARTED SIX YEARS AGO!

WHEN IT WAS THE THREE OF US LEAVING FOR VAMPIRE MOUNTAIN.

GU (MMPH)

ZA (WAVE)

FOR NOW, LET US SIMPLY WALK.

WE CAN DECIDE LATER.

GU (TUG)

WHERE ARE WE GOING... THIS TIME?

COULD BE TOMORROW, COULD BE MONTHS AWAY...

SO, WHEN WILL WE SEE THIS VAMPANEZE LORD NEXT?

WHAT COMES, WE TAKE. ON-WARD !!!

THREE CHANCES REMAIN TO FELL THE DREAD LORD OF THE VAM-PANEZE...

HUNTERS OF THE DUSK 7 - END

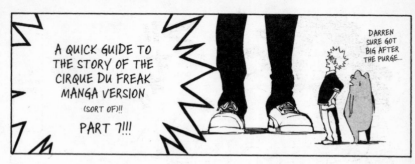

A QUICK GUIDE TO THE STORY OF THE CIRQUE DU FREAK MANGA VERSION (SORT OF)!! PART 7!!!

DARREN SURE GOT BIG AFTER THE PURGE...

NOW THAT MY ENTIRE WEEK IS FILLED WITH DRAFTING AND DRAWING A CHAPTER, CLEANING MY WORKPLACE, AND DOING LAUNDRY, SHE'S THE ONLY THING THAT KEEPS ME GOING.

SHUZAA (ZESHH)

IN THE AUTHOR'S COMMENTS FOR THIS VOLUME, I MENTIONED NANA THE BORDER COLLIE. BOY IS SHE CUTE!

PART 1: RELAX-ATION

ARE YOU GOING THROUGH THE PURGE TOO? YOU USED TO BE SO SMALL!

EVERY TIME I RETURN TO MY PARENTS' HOUSE, SHE'S A LITTLE BIT BIGGER. IT'S A JOY TO SEE HER GROW BEFORE MY EYES.

ZUSHI (LUMPH)

WHAT I LEARNED LATER IS THAT SHE'S AN ENGLISH BREED, AND DARREN-SAN'S FAMILY HAS ONE AS WELL. WHAT A STRANGE COINCIDENCE!

THERE ARE LITTLE PICTURES IN THE JAPANESE PROSE EDITION OF THE EXTRA SHORT STORIES.

WHEN I FINALLY RETURN HOME AND FALL ASLEEP IN THE FAMILY ROOM, SHE ACTS AS A WAKE-UP CALL IN THE MORNING!

HER PASSIONATE KISSES BRISKLY WAKE ME FROM MY SLUMBER.

GYAAA (AAAGH!)

BERO BERO (CLICK) BERO

ZUOOO
(LOOM)

MY LADY!

OF COURSE, IN THIS VOLUME WE ARE FIRST INTRODUCED TO THE ULTRA-IMPORTANT CHARACTER OF EVANNA.

PART 2: EVANNA'S DESIGN

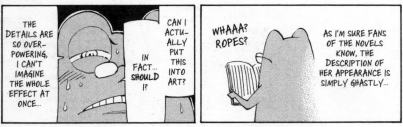

THE DETAILS ARE SO OVER-POWERING, I CAN'T IMAGINE THE WHOLE EFFECT AT ONCE...

IN FACT... **SHOULD** I?

CAN I ACTU-ALLY PUT THIS INTO ART?

WHAAA? ROPES?

AS I'M SURE FANS OF THE NOVELS KNOW, THE DESCRIPTION OF HER APPEARANCE IS SIMPLY GHASTLY...

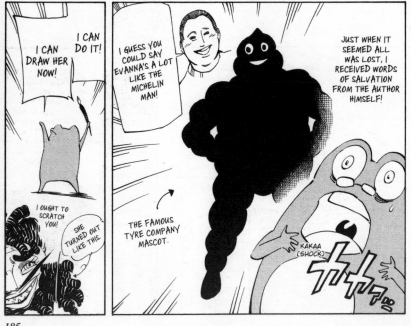

I CAN DRAW HER NOW!

I CAN DO IT!

I GUESS YOU COULD SAY EVANNA'S A LOT LIKE THE MICHELIN MAN!

JUST WHEN IT SEEMED ALL WAS LOST, I RECEIVED WORDS OF SALVATION FROM THE AUTHOR HIMSELF!

I OUGHT TO SCRATCH YOU!

SHE TURNED OUT LIKE THIS.

THE FAMOUS TYRE COMPANY MASCOT.

KAKAA (SHOCK)

THAT WAS JUST THE START OF A BEWILDERING, CHAOTIC, DESPERATE RESEARCH EXPEDITION!

FINALLY, THE IMPORTANT PART! IN JANUARY OF 2008, IN ORDER TO MAKE THE CIRQUE DU FREAK MANGA MORE REALISTIC THAN EVER BEFORE, I TOOK A TRIP...

...TO ENGLAND!!

PART 3: TRIP TO ENGLAND

OOOOH!

オオー！

WE RODE ONE OF THE FAMOUS LONDON TAXIS OUT OF HEATHROW AIRPORT TO A HOTEL IN THE CITY.

ENGLAND IS COLD! BUT WAIT...I FEEL LIKE IT MIGHT HAVE BEEN COLDER IN TOKYO. IT ACTUALLY FEELS NICE HERE.

TWELVE-HOUR FLIGHT? BIG DEAL!

DAY ONE

I DECIDED ON A TIME AND PLACE TO MEET MY EDITOR, AND WE HEADED FOR THE FAMOUS JUNCTION, PICCADILLY CIRCUS!!

WHOO-HOO!

IT WAS ALREADY DARK OUTSIDE (ENGLAND'S WINTER DAYS ARE VERY SHORT), BUT I WANTED TO GET STARTED TAKING PHOTOS.

GARA (ROLL)

ガラガラ

GARA

AND IT'S ALL BECAUSE OF MY EDITOR'S SUPPORT...

THIS IS GREAT!

I CAN'T BELIEVE I'M REALLY IN LONDON!

THE ROWS UPON ROWS OF STONE BUILDINGS SEEM TO PRESS THE WEIGHT OF HISTORY ONTO YOU.

DON (THUMP)

OH! I'M SORRY...

LONDON IS NOTHING SHORT OF BEAUTIFUL.

...AND MY GENEROUS CHIEF EDITOR! THANK YOU!!

EVERYONE WAS SO FASHIONABLE AND COOL!

WATCH WHERE YOU'RE BLOODY WALKIN'!

EEEK!

AND OF COURSE, I WAS SURROUNDED BY LONDONERS!

Nobody treated me like this!

EVERY ONE OF THESE PHOTOS I TAKE WILL TURN INTO THE FLESH AND BLOOD OF THE CIRQUE DU FREAK MANGA!!

BASHA

BASHA

I SNAPPED THE SHUTTER AS THOUGH IN A DREAM.

BASHA (CLICK)

ZAAAAA (FSHHHHH)

UM...WHERE AM I?

WELL! THAT SHOULD DO IT. TIME TO HEAD BACK TO THE HOTEL!

AFTER TAKING A MOUNTAIN OF PICTURES, I FELT TRULY FULFILLED.

THIS SILLY FROG HAS MANAGED TO GET HIMSELF LOST ON THE VERY FIRST DAY OF HIS TRIP! WHAT WILL HAPPEN NEXT!?

THE NEXT THING I KNEW, HEAVY RAINDROPS WERE FALLING FROM THE THICK CLOUDS THAT ENVELOPED THE CITY...

WHEW!

to be continued!!

CREATOR COMMENTS

VOLUME

VAMPIRES. IT'S HARD TO IMAGINE FINDING A MORE FASCINATING FICTIONAL CREATURE IN THE ENTIRE WORLD. IMAGINE WHAT IT WOULD BE LIKE TO BE A VAMPIRE, BOYS AND GIRLS . . . AND JOIN DARREN ON THIS JOURNEY THROUGH THE EERIE DARK OF NIGHT.

ENJOY ARTIST TAKAHIRO ARAI'S COMMENTARY FROM THE ORIGINAL DUST JACKETS OF THE FIRST SEVEN VOLUMES OF *DARREN SHAN!*

VOLUME

VOLUME

I'VE BEEN COLLECTING PHOTOS OF EUROPE FOR REFERENCE USE. WHEN I LOOK AT THEM, I THINK "WHAT FANTASY!" THE ANCIENT CASTLES THAT SEEM SURE TO HARBOUR GHOSTS, DARK FORESTS FILLED WITH FAIRY SPIRITS . . . IT'S SUCH A BEWITCHING PLACE.

I FINALLY MANAGED TO FIND A JAR OF PICKLED ONIONS AT AN IMPORTED FOODS STORE. RATHER THAN BEING SLICED, I WAS SURPRISED TO SEE THAT THEY WERE CUTE, LITTLE, WHOLE ONIONS. WHEN I POPPED ONE INTO MY MOUTH, A POWERFULLY SOUR TASTE SPREAD ACROSS MY TONGUE.

WELL, WELL, WELL! I HAD THE PLEASURE OF MEETING WITH THE AUTHOR, MR. DARREN SHAN HIMSELF, WHEN HE VISITED JAPAN FOR AN AUTOGRAPH SIGNING TOUR!! EEEEEEEK!! I WILL WRITE MORE ABOUT THIS EXPERIENCE IN THE BONUS MATERIAL OF VOLUME SIX. IT WAS A DREAM COME TRUE . . .

ODDLY ENOUGH, FOR AS LONG AS I CAN REMEMBER, WHILE I'M WORKING ON THE SCRIPT FOR THE MANGA AND PLANNING EACH PANEL, I DON'T GET HUNGRY. OR AT LEAST, I DON'T NOTICE IT. I BET I COULD GO TWO OR THREE DAYS WITHOUT EATING IF I WAS JUST DOING THIS STAGE OF THE MANGA PROCESS. BUT WHEN I'M ACTUALLY DRAWING UP THE FINISHED PAGES, I'VE ALWAYS GOT TO HAVE SOMETHING AT HAND TO NIBBLE ON. NO MATTER WHAT, THERE'S SOME BAG OF SNACKS AT MY SIDE. I WONDER IF I'VE GOT CONCENTRATION ISSUES...